THE
NO-
GLUTEN
Cookbook

THE NO-GLUTEN Cookbook

Delicious recipes to make
your mouth water . . .
all gluten-free!

Series Editor: Kimberly A. Tessmer, R.D., L.D.

Adams Media
Avon, Massachusetts

Copyright © 2007, F+W Publications, Inc.
All rights reserved. This book, or parts thereof, may not be reproduced
in any form without permission from the publisher; exceptions are made
for brief excerpts used in published reviews.

Published by
Adams Media,
an F+W Publications Company
57 Littlefield Street
Avon, MA 02322
www.adamsmedia.com

ISBN 10: 1-59869-089-2
ISBN 13: 978-1-59869-089-7

Printed in the United States of America.

J I H G F E D C B A

Library of Congress Cataloging-in-Publication Data
The no-gluten cookbook.
p.   cm.
ISBN-13: 978-1-59869-089-7
ISBN-10: 1-59869-089-2
1. Gluten-free diet—Recipes. 2. Wheat-free diet—Recipes. I. Adams Media
RM237.87.N644 2006
641.5'638—dc22
2006028204

This publication is designed to provide accurate and authoritative information with regard to the subject matter covered. It is sold with the understanding that the publisher is not engaged in rendering legal, accounting, or other professional advice. If legal advice or other expert assistance is required, the services of a competent professional person should be sought.
—From a *Declaration of Principles* jointly adopted by a Committee of the American Bar Association and a Committee of Publishers and Associations

Many of the designations used by manufacturers and sellers to distinguish their product are claimed as trademarks. Where those designations appear in this book and Adams Media was aware of a trademark claim, the designations have been printed with initial capital letters.

Contains portions of material adapted or abridged from *The Everything® Gluten-Free Cookbook* by Nancy T. Maar and Rick Marx, ©2005, F+W Publications, Inc.

The No-Gluten Cookbook is intended as a reference volume only, not as a medical manual. In light of the complex, individual, and specific nature of heath problems, this book is not intended to replace professional medical advice. The ideas, procedures, and suggestions in this book are intended to supplement, not replace, the advice of a trained medical professional. Consult your physician before adopting the suggestions in this book. The author and publisher disclaim any liability arising directly or indirectly from the use of this book.

This book is available at quantity discounts for bulk purchases.
For information, please call 1-800-289-0963.

Introduction

The world of gluten-free foods can be perplexing to say the least! For people with celiac disease and other conditions that require a gluten-free diet, following this daily eating regime is crucial to preventing complications and serious symptoms associated with the condition. In today's world of gluten-laden foods there can be potential threats at every turn, including your own kitchen. Each ingredient and product consumed needs to be closely scrutinized and analyzed for any trace of gluten (barley, rye, oats, and wheat), which means learning to properly interpret food labels. To complicate matters even more, there is a long list of hidden and unfamiliar ingredients used in foods that can contain gluten even though their name may not make it obvious.

The good news is that there are plenty of tasty and healthy alternative foods and ingredients that are perfectly safe to use on a gluten-free diet. The key to getting started is acquiring essential education from a health professional such as a dietitian and stocking your kitchen with "safe" foods and helpful cookbooks. New food options are becoming more readily available and more easily accessible every day as manufacturers realize the increased need for gluten-free products. The Internet has become an outlet to purchase specialized foods as well as a way to obtain information and support. It is extremely important to note that manufacturers often change ingredients or suppliers for their food products, so carefully reading labels on a regular basis and contacting companies if you're in doubt is essential to ensuring that the foods you eat remain gluten-free. You can never let your guard down when following a gluten-free diet. However, the process becomes easier as you learn how to interpret information and to take control of your life. *The No-Gluten Cookbook* is an easy-to-use guide to include in your arsenal of information to help make your life a little easier and a lot tastier!

Important Note: Many foods within this cookbook are marked GF (gluten-free). The ingredients of these foods must be analyzed by brand to ensure they are gluten-free. All companies create different versions of different foods, so you need to check labels carefully and never assume that a food is gluten-free. It is a smart idea to get in the habit of checking *all* foods, whether you know they are gluten-free or not, including those within each recipe of this book.

Happy Cooking!

Understanding Gluten-Free Diets and Cooking

chapter one

I s a gluten-free (GF) diet important for your lifestyle? If you have a food allergy or the autoimmune disorder known as celiac disease, it may be important for you to take charge of your life and begin a new food regimen. Most people don't know about gluten-free diets until they are told they need to be on them!

What Is a Gluten Disorder?

About 1 in 133 people suffer from celiac disease, and health organizations say 2 percent to 2.5 percent of the general population suffer from a food allergy—or between 6 million and 7 million Americans. The difference between a food allergy and celiac disease is that the latter, also known as celiac sprue, is an autoimmune disorder, like diabetes.

Unlike other autoimmune diseases, however, physicians know the trigger for celiac disease: gluten, which provokes an immune response that causes the body to attack itself. Two key components come into play in celiac disease: genes and environmental factors.

Celiac disease is an intestinal disorder caused by the intolerance of some individuals to gluten, a protein in wheat, rye, barley, and some other grains. Gluten irritates the intestinal lining, interfering with the absorption of nutrients and water. Unlike certain food allergies, celiac disease is not "grown out of," and those with the disease must maintain constant vigilance to keep their diet gluten-free. Untreated, the disease can lead to severe complications and potential long-term illness. The disease is permanent, and damage to the small intestine will occur every time gluten is consumed, regardless of whether symptoms are present. Reactions among people who suffer from this disease vary, but they are inevitable. The only treatment is strict adherence to a 100 percent gluten-free diet.

Maintaining a healthy gluten-free lifestyle involves eating a well-balanced, gluten-free diet that is high in protein and normal in fats. Common nutrient shortages among people with celiac disease include deficiencies in calcium; the vitamin B complex; and vitamins A, C, D, K, and E. It is important for the celiac to eat a carefully balanced diet to ensure that he or she is getting all the vitamins the body needs.

So, What Can I Eat?

The gluten-free diet involves totally eliminating the ingestion of all items containing the proteins found in wheat, rye, barley, and the many related grains. Before you turn to a gluten-free diet, make sure you see your physician and determine if eliminating gluten is right for you. Starting the diet without complete testing is not recommended and makes diagnosis later more difficult. Always be safe rather than sorry.

Once you've made the decision to be gluten-free, you can purchase ingredients at natural food stores, online, and at some grocery stores. Fresh fruits, meats, and veggies are a great place to start—always remember, if they are fresh, they are gluten-free. If the food is manufactured or prepared, chances are it is not. In building a gluten-free diet plan, remove wheat grain products, including the obvious—breads, cakes, and cookies—and the not so obvious, such as products with wheat starch or other gluten-containing grain derivatives.

Every person with celiac disease must become a bit of a chemist. Preparing delicious gluten-free foods takes practice, diligence, and experimentation. Audrey Birnbaum, M.D., a physician affiliated with Northern Westchester Hospital in Mount Kisco, New York, who specializes in pediatric gastrointestinal disorders and food allergies, recommends purchasing products on the Internet or from health food stores, and enlisting the assistance of a dietitian. She says that it's usually easy to make the whole house comfortable with a gluten-free diet.

"Try to stay as pure as possible," Dr. Birnbaum says. "Is it OK to cheat? I tell patients: Bring your own gluten-free cupcakes. You don't have to be obsessive, but you should be an intelligent consumer."

That includes reading labels, checking Web sites, and staying informed on medical developments. Some supplements may be required to replace the nutrients lost by eliminating wheat and gluten from the diet. For example, the body's iron requirements might go up.

How Should I Shop for Food?

Supermarkets, especially the natural food specialty stores, carry a variety of gluten-free foods. Visit your local natural foods store or go to the Web. Talk to friends or support groups who have had experience with celiac disease or food allergies. Find out all the different flours you can use, and maximize the resources at your fingertips.

To put together a gluten-free pantry, make sure you have four kinds of flour. We recommend rice, corn, chestnut (for desserts), and quinoa (for protein). You'll need an electric blender, a mixer, and a food processor, items that any cook would find useful but that are essential for the preparation of gluten-free food. Stock up on plenty of fresh vegetables, lots of good meats, and high-quality seafood. Avoid preseasoned foods, as flour may have been added to the seasoning mix.

Scott Adams, founder of celiac.com and the Gluten Free Mall, offers an online site that sells a wide variety of gluten-free products. Scott, who has celiac disease, started the business in 1996 to give consumers greater options in buying gluten-free products. Scott recommends that consumers prepare their lists by consulting support groups and doing research at home and online. His site and others like it often provide links to manufacturers, products, and product information.

Always keep alert when buying food with these three tips in mind:

- When in a grocery store, make sure to read the labels.
- Open your mouth and ask questions everywhere you go.
- Once you've gone gluten-free, to share your new food lifestyle.

Can I Live a Gluten-Free Life Happily?

Don't feel deprived—gluten-free food is as delicious as any other. For example, food fried in deep fat the southern way has no wheat flour—it's made with corn flour and/or cornmeal. Dip meat, chicken, veggies, and shrimp in corn flour and egg, then in cornmeal, and you've got a crunchy, delicious, deep-fried meal.

A trip to an ethnic grocery store may open up many new sources of delicious meals. Corn flour, found in Latin American groceries, works well. Risotto, a staple in Italian cooking, is a delicious alternative to pasta. Try flour substitutes in traditional recipes.

Despite a good pasta-making machine, commercial gluten-free pasta is much more sensible than homemade. Try one of the gluten-free pastas available from your health or Asian food store and online retailers.

Remember, experimentation is part of the process, so don't get discouraged. When you start cooking, you may not get it right the first time. Keep trying until you do get it right.

Be creative. Vary ingredients and quantities and follow the recipes in this book for success. Bon appetit!

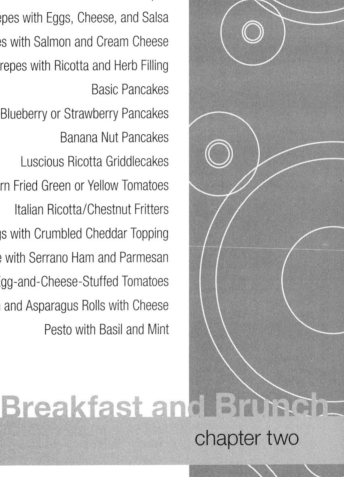

Breakfast and Brunch

chapter two

Chestnut Flour Crepes

Makes 12 crepes

2 eggs
1 cup milk
½ teaspoon salt
½ cup chestnut flour
½ cup rice flour
2 teaspoons sugar (optional)
2 tablespoons butter, melted
(plus more for pan)

Chestnut flour is sweet and nutty, making the most delicious crepes you can imagine. You can stuff them with fruit and whipped cream, or with savory fillings.

1. Whirl the eggs, milk, and salt in your food processor. With the motor on low, slowly add the flours, stopping occasionally to scrape down the sides of the jar.

2. Add the sugar if you are making sweet crepes with sweet filling; omit if you are going to fill them with savory delights.

3. Pour in melted butter and whirl until well blended. Pour mixture by half-cupfuls into a nonstick sauté pan to which you've added a dot of butter. Tilt the pan to spread the batter thinly.

4. Fry the crepes on medium heat, turning until browned on both sides; place on waxed paper and sprinkle with a bit of rice flour to prevent them from sticking.

5. When the crepes are done, you can fill them right away or store them in the refrigerator or freezer for later use.

Using Nonstick Sauté Pans

Nonstick pans take all of the grief out of making crepes. However, even if your pan is quite new, it's important to use a bit of butter for insurance and extra flavor. Keep the pan well buttered and you have an almost foolproof method for making perfect crepes.

Chestnut Crepes with Prosciutto and Peach Sauce

If you can't find mascarpone cheese, use cream cheese. You can make the crepes and sauce and fill the crepes in advance. Just heat everything up at the last moment.

1. Mix the cornstarch in cold water until very smooth. Place in a saucepan with the peaches, lemon juice, hot sauce, and sugar. You may need to add some more water if the peaches are not very juicy. Bring to a boil, stirring constantly, until very thick and syrupy. Taste for seasonings and add black pepper to taste.

2. Preheat oven to 300°F.

3. Lay the crepes on a baking sheet and spread with the cheese. Place a slice of ham over each and roll up. Use GF nonstick spray on a pie pan or baking dish.

4. Arrange the rolls, seam-side down, in the pan and bake for 10 to 15 minutes or until the crepe rolls are hot. Serve with the peach syrup.

Serves 4

2 tablespoons cornstarch
¼ cup cold water
2 peaches, blanched, peeled, and sliced
Juice of ½ lemon
1 teaspoon GF hot red pepper sauce, or to taste
½ cup sugar
8 small Chestnut Flour Crepes (see page 6)
Plenty of freshly ground black pepper
8 teaspoons mascarpone cheese or cream cheese
8 paper-thin slices of GF prosciutto ham

Buckwheat Pancakes with Sour Cream and Caviar

Serves 4 to 6

2 eggs
¾ cup buttermilk
½ cup rice flour
½ cup pure buckwheat flour
  (wheat-free)
1 teaspoon sugar
1 teaspoon salt
1 tablespoon GF baking
  powder
½ teaspoon baking soda
1 tablespoon butter, melted,
  plus 2 tablespoons
  for frying pancakes
1 cup GF sour cream
2 ounces GF salmon caviar

You can serve this "Russian breakfast" at any time of day! These should be made small, about 1½ to 2 inches in diameter.

1. Whisk eggs and buttermilk together. Slowly beat in rice flour, buckwheat flour, sugar, salt, baking powder, baking soda, and melted butter. You may have to add more milk to get a thick, creamy consistency.

2. Set stove at medium-high and butter your griddle or frying pan. Drop ¼ to ⅓ cup batter onto the griddle. Turn when you see bubbles coming up through the batter, about 3 minutes, and then fry for another 2 minutes. It's OK to peek. Serve with a dollop of sour cream and caviar.

Cooking with Buckwheat

Buckwheat has a flavor all its own. It's both nutty and slightly tart. Even though it contains the word "wheat" in its name, it is gluten-free and actually is related not to wheat but to the rhubarb plant. The more you work with buckwheat, the more respect you will have for it. You can dress buckwheat pancakes with all kinds of sauces, such as mushroom, grilled vegetables, and melted cheese.

Be aware that some companies mix buckwheat flour with wheat flour to lessen its strong taste. Be sure you use pure buckwheat flour in your recipes to ensure it is gluten-free.

Mushroom and Cheese Crepes

This filling is excellent for brunch, lunch, or a light supper. You can vary the herbs.

1. Sauté the mushrooms in oil until softened. Add the sage leaves and salt and pepper. In a bowl, mix the mushrooms with the ricotta and egg.

2. Preheat oven to 350°F.

3. Lay out the crepes. Put a tablespoon of filling on one side of each. Roll and put in a baking dish. Cover with Basic Cream Sauce and sprinkle with Parmesan cheese.

4. Bake for 20 minutes, and serve hot.

Makes 12 crepes

12 Chestnut Flour Crepes
   (see page 6) or Corn
   Crepes (see page 11)
2 cups mushrooms, brushed
   clean and chopped
2 tablespoons olive oil
6 sage leaves, shredded
Salt and pure black pepper
   to taste
½ cup ricotta cheese
1 egg, lightly beaten
1 recipe Basic Cream Sauce
   (see page 176)
½ cup Parmesan cheese

Sweet and Spicy Apple-Cinnamon Crepes

Makes 12 crepes

2 large tart apples, such
  as Granny Smith, peeled,
  cored, and chopped
1 tablespoon butter
1 teaspoon cinnamon
¼ teaspoon ground cloves
2 tablespoons brown sugar, or
  to taste
4 ounces cream cheese, at
  room temperature
12 Chestnut Flour Crepes
  (see page 6), with sugar
Whipped cream or GF vanilla
  ice cream

Just the aroma of this perfect weekend brunch dish will make you hungry. It's going to get the kids out of bed too.

1. Sauté the apples in butter for 20 minutes. Stir in cinnamon, cloves, and sugar. Blend the cream cheese into the hot mixture.

2. Preheat oven to 350°F.

3. Lay out crepes and place a spoonful of filling on each. Roll them and place in a baking dish prepared with GF nonstick spray.

4. Bake in oven until hot, about 8 to 10 minutes. Serve with whipped cream or GF vanilla ice cream.

Corn Crepes

As with the Chestnut Flour Crepes (see page 6), you can make these in advance and store them in the refrigerator or freezer.

1. Place the eggs, milk, and salt in your food processor and whirl until smooth. With the motor on low, slowly add the flour and spoon in the sugar if you are making sweet crepes. Scrape down the sides of the jar often. Add melted butter.

2. Heat a nonstick pan over medium heat and add a spoonful of vegetable oil. Pour in the batter to make the crepes. Tilt the pan to spread the batter evenly.

3. Place crepes on sheets of waxed paper that have been dusted with extra corn flour.

4. To store, place in a plastic bag in refrigerator or freezer. You can stuff these with GF salsa, jack cheese, and GF sour cream, or with mashed fruit such as strawberries.

Storing Crepes

To store crepes, simply put a bit of corn flour on sheets of waxed paper and stack the crepes individually. Then put the whole stack in a plastic bag and store in a refrigerator or freezer.

Makes 12 crepes

2 eggs
1 cup milk or buttermilk
1 teaspoon salt or to taste
1 cup corn flour (available in Latino markets with slaked lime)
2 teaspoons sugar (optional)
2 tablespoons butter, melted
Vegetable oil for frying crepes

Corn Crepes with Eggs, Cheese, and Salsa

Makes 12 crepes

1 recipe Corn Crepes (see
    page 11)
12 thin slices jack or pepper
    jack cheese
12 eggs, poached or fried
    sunny-side up
12 teaspoons GF salsa
12 teaspoons grated Parme-
    san cheese

These Mexican-style crepes make a fantastic brunch!

1. Place the crepes on cookie sheets that you've prepared with GF nonstick spray. Put a slice of cheese on each crepe. Place one egg on each piece of cheese. Spoon a bit of salsa on top of each egg.

2. Preheat the broiler to 400°F. Sprinkle the crepes with Parmesan cheese and broil for about 5 minutes, until cheese is hot and starting to melt.

3. If you wish, you can put the jack cheese on top of the eggs, and serve the salsa on the side.

Corn Crepes with Salmon and Cream Cheese

Love the taste of smoked salmon and cream cheese? These crepes will hit the spot. You can substitute unsweetened whipped cream for the cream cheese.

1. Toast the crepes on a baking sheet under the broiler at 350°F for about 5 minutes. Spread with cream cheese.

2. Place the sliced salmon over the cheese and let people help themselves to onion slices and condiments.

Serves 4

12 Corn Crepes (see page 11)
4 ounces cream cheese, room temperature
4 ounces sliced GF smoked salmon
½ sweet onion, sliced thin
Condiments such as GF horseradish, chopped chives, GF mustard

Corn Is a Crucial Food

Cornmeal is an ancient grain, first raised in South and Central America. It made its way north via seeds passed by native tribes. By the time the Pilgrims got to Plymouth, corn was a staple in North America. It's hardy, sustaining, and a "hot" food, warming the body. Without corn, or maize, supplied by sympathetic Indians, settlers in this country would not have survived.

Corn Crepes with Ricotta and Herb Filling

Makes 12 crepes

1½ cups ricotta cheese

2 eggs

¼ cup finely grated Parmesan cheese

Salt and freshly ground black pepper, to taste

¼ cup basil leaves (or your favorite herbs), finely chopped

1 recipe Corn Crepes (see page 11)

1 recipe Basic Cream Sauce (see page 176)

1 cup shredded white American cheese

Try a variety of herbs in the filling, such as fresh basil, sage, oregano, or chopped rosemary.

1. In your food processor, whirl the ricotta cheese, eggs, Parmesan cheese, salt and pepper, and basil.

2. Preheat oven to 325°F. Lay crepes out and prepare a large baking dish with GF nonstick spray. Place a tablespoon of filling on the end of each crepe and roll. Arrange them in the baking dish.

3. Pour sauce over crepes. Sprinkle with white American cheese. Bake for 25 minutes. Serve hot.

Herbs and Spices

People often confuse herbs with spices. Herbs are green and are the leaves of plants—the only herb (in Western cooking) that is a flower is lavender. Frequently used herbs include parsley, basil, oregano, thyme, rosemary, cilantro, and mint. Spices are roots, tubers, barks, or berries. These include pepper, cinnamon, nutmeg, allspice, cumin, turmeric, ginger, cardamom, and coriander. For the gluten-free diet, be sure to use pure herbs and spices.

Basic Pancakes

For a lighter pancake, separate the eggs and beat the whites stiffly. These pancakes are great with mashed fresh peaches, strawberries, and/or blueberries.

1. In the bowl of a food processor, whirl all of the liquid ingredients. Slowly add the baking powder and flour.

2. Heat griddle pan or large frying pan to medium. Drop a teaspoon of butter on it; when the butter sizzles, start pouring on the batter to about 2 inches in diameter.

3. When bubbles come to the top, turn the pancakes and continue to fry until golden brown. Place on a plate in a warm oven to keep warm while you make the others.

Flour Substitutions

Try substituting rice or potato flour in some recipes. Chickpea flour also makes an excellent savory pancake. You have so many choices—it's fun to exercise them.

Makes 16 pancakes

½ cup milk
2 eggs
1½ tablespoons butter, melted
1 tablespoon GF baking powder
1 cup rice flour (or substitute corn, chickpea, or tapioca flour)
Extra butter for frying pancakes

Blueberry or Strawberry Pancakes

Makes 12 pancakes

½ pint blueberries or
   strawberries
1 tablespoon sugar
1 teaspoon orange zest
1 recipe Basic Pancakes batter
   (see page 15)

Fruit on, or inside, pancakes is classic, healthy, and delicious.

1. In a bowl, mix the fruit, sugar, and orange zest. Mash with a potato masher or pestle.

2. Heat griddle to medium. Add butter. Pour pancake batter to desired size and spoon some berries on top of each cake.

3. Turn when bubbles rise to the top of the cakes, and brown other side. You will get some caramelization from the sugar and fruit—it's delicious. Top with more berries and whipped cream.

Freezing Fruit in Its Prime

There's nothing like blueberry pie in January, and I'm not talking about the fruit that comes all ready and loaded with sugar syrup in a can. When fresh blueberries are available, just rinse a quart and dry on paper towels. Place the berries on a cookie sheet in the freezer for a half hour and then put them in a plastic bag for future use. Beware of canned pie fillings that are thickened with flour and therefore not gluten-free.

Banana Nut Pancakes

The bananas can be either sliced onto the cakes or mashed and incorporated into the batter.

1. Whirl the banana in a food processor until smooth.

2. Heat pan or griddle over medium heat. Add butter and pour the batter a half cup at a time. Sprinkle nuts on top of each cake.

3. Turn when the pancakes begin to bubble on top. Place on a warm platter. Serve with freshly whipped cream.

Serves 4

1 banana
Extra butter for frying cakes
1 recipe Basic Pancakes batter
  (see page 15)
1 cup coarsely chopped
  walnuts
1 cup heavy cream whipped
  with 1 tablespoon sugar

Luscious Ricotta Griddlecakes

Makes 12 griddlecakes

1 cup ricotta cheese
2 whole eggs plus 1 egg yolk
⅓ cup plus 1 tablespoon rice
    or tapioca flour
1 teaspoon vanilla extract
1 teaspoon baking soda
½ teaspoon salt
⅛ teaspoon nutmeg
⅛ teaspoon cinnamon
2 tablespoons unsalted butter,
    melted
Extra butter for sautéing the
    cakes

Preparing the batter in your blender makes it velvety smooth. You can serve with fruit, or dress with a berry coulis. The ricotta adds protein.

1. Whirl the ingredients in your blender, adding them in the order given above, finishing with the melted butter.

2. Set your griddle over medium heat and melt a liberal amount of butter on it. When the butter foams, start dropping cakes by ¼ cupfuls on the griddle.

3. After 4 minutes, turn and cook the other side. Stack on a platter in a low (200°F) oven to keep warm until ready to serve. Serve with fruit, syrup, or a fruit coulis.

Southern Fried Green or Yellow Tomatoes

Use tomatoes that are very firm. They usually aren't very large, so count on two per person. Serve with thick slices of GF country ham or GF Irish bacon.

1. Spread the flour mixed with salt and pepper on one sheet of waxed paper and the cornmeal on another. Place the whisked eggs in a bowl between the two.

2. Dip the tomato slices first in the flour, then in the egg, and then coat them with cornmeal.

3. Heat ½ inch of oil in a frying pan to 350°F. Slide the tomato slices in and fry for 4 minutes or until well browned. Turn and finish frying.

4. Drain on paper towels. Serve as a side dish with eggs and GF bacon. As an extra fillip, you can add a dollop of GF sour cream to each tomato slice.

Serves 4

1 cup corn flour
Coarsely ground pure black
  pepper to taste
1 cup cornmeal
2 whole eggs whisked in a
  large flat soup bowl
8 green or yellow tomatoes,
  cores trimmed, cut in
  ⅓-inch slices
Oil for frying
1 teaspoon salt

Italian Ricotta/Chestnut Fritters

Serves 4

2 eggs
½ cup sugar
1 teaspoon vanilla extract
1 teaspoon baking soda
1 cup ricotta cheese
½ cup chestnut flour
½ cup rice flour
Vegetable oil for frying
Powdered sugar to dust
    fritters

This is a traditional Italian recipe. These fritters are a wonderful side dish at brunch with GF bacon or GF ham. They're easier to make than home fries.

1. Beat the eggs and sugar until thick. Slowly add the rest of the ingredients except the vegetable oil and the powdered sugar. Cover the bowl and let stand for 1 hour.

2. Heat 2 inches of oil over medium-high heat to 375°F. Drop the fritters by tablespoonfuls into the oil. Do not overfill the pot. Fry for about 2 minutes, turning as they brown.

3. Drain on brown paper or paper towels and dust with powdered sugar.

Shirred Eggs with Crumbled Cheddar Topping

These are just plain cute and appealing. For an extra touch, you can place a thin slice of tomato in the bottom of each ramekin.

1. Preheat the oven to 350°F. Prepare 12 small 4-ounce ramekins or 6 larger 6-ounce ones with GF nonstick spray. Place the ramekins on a cookie sheet. Break 1 egg into each of 12 small or 2 eggs into each of 6 large ramekins.

2. Sprinkle the eggs with salt and pepper and dot with butter.

3. Sprinkle with Cheddar and bake for 8 to 12 minutes. Serve immediately.

An Elegant Touch

If you are having a crowd of people to brunch, place ramekins on a cookie sheet and bake for 10 minutes. Then, serve with a big bowl of fruit on the side. You can use glass custard cups, but individual ramekins made of white porcelain are more elegant.

Serves 6

12 extra-large eggs
Salt and pure black pepper
    to taste
4 tablespoons butter
¾ cup grated Cheddar cheese

Ricotta Torte with Serrano Ham and Parmesan

Serves 6

2 shallots, peeled and minced
2 tablespoons butter
3 eggs
1 pound ricotta cheese
½ cup Parmesan cheese, grated
¼ cup GF serrano or GF prosciutto ham, chopped fine
4 tablespoons butter, melted
1 teaspoon dried oregano
⅛ teaspoon nutmeg
Salt and pure black pepper to taste

If you can't find serrano ham, substitute prosciutto ham. Do not, however, use low-fat ricotta—it just doesn't do the trick.

1. Sauté the shallots in butter and place in a pie pan that you have prepared with GF non-stick spray. Preheat the oven to 325°F.

2. Beat the eggs and add the rest of the ingredients, beating all the time. Pour into prepared pie pan and bake for 35 minutes, or until set and golden. Cut into wedges and serve.

Spicy Egg-and-Cheese-Stuffed Tomatoes

This is a fine way to use up the end-of-summer tomatoes in your garden.

1. Cut the tops off the tomatoes, core, and, using a melon baller, scoop out seeds and pulp. Place the tomatoes on a baking sheet covered with parchment paper or sprayed with GF nonstick spray. Mix the spices and oregano together, using half on the insides of the tomatoes, saving the rest for topping.

2. Preheat the oven to 350°F.

3. Sauté the garlic in the butter. While it's cooking, mix together the salt, black pepper, cayenne pepper, oregano, and cumin in a small bowl.

4. Rub the insides of the tomatoes with the spice mixture, saving a bit aside for the eggs. Spoon the butter and garlic mixture into the tomatoes. Sprinkle with half of the remaining spice mixture.

5. Break an egg into each tomato. Sprinkle with the rest of the spice mixture. Loosely spoon the cheese over the eggs, then sprinkle 1 teaspoon cornbread crumbs over each tomato. Bake for 20 minutes. The tomatoes should still be firm, the eggs soft, the cheese melted, and the bread crumbs browned.

Priceless Heirlooms

There are good tomatoes in the supermarket and good tomatoes in cans, but the best tomatoes are homegrown. Recently there has been a trend toward growing ancient varieties of tomato. These "heirlooms," as they are called, have more flavor, sweetness paired with acid, then ordinary tomatoes do. You can buy the seeds and grow them yourself, and some green markets carry them too.

Serves 4

8 medium tomatoes
2 cloves garlic, minced or put through a garlic press
4 tablespoons butter
1 teaspoon salt
1 teaspoon pure black pepper
1 teaspoon cayenne pepper
1 teaspoon dried oregano
1 teaspoon cumin powder
8 eggs
½ cup grated Monterey jack or Cheddar cheese
8 teaspoons GF cornbread crumbs

Ham and Asparagus Rolls with Cheese

Serves 6

1 10-oz. package frozen
   asparagus
½ pound GF smoked ham,
   sliced thin
½ pound white American
   cheese, sliced thin
1 recipe Creamy Cheddar
   Sauce with Ham and Sherry
   (see page 177)

This is excellent for a cool morning. It's tasty enough to get things going, and hearty enough to stay with you for a morning of skiing or sledding.

1. Preheat oven to 350°F. Drop frozen asparagus in boiling water for 1 minute and dry on paper towels. Lay out the slices of ham. Place a slice of cheese and then an asparagus spear on each ham slice. Roll up and secure with toothpicks if necessary.

2. Place the rolls in a glass baking pan that you've treated with GF nonstick spray. Pour cheese sauce over the top.

3. Bake for 25 minutes or until lightly browned on top and heated through. Serve hot.

Pesto with Basil and Mint

This variation on an old classic is savory with hard-boiled or poached eggs, over GF pasta, or as a condiment with cold meat or poultry. It's very good over sliced cold chicken.

Put all ingredients in blender and whirl until smooth. Serve as a side dish over GF pasta or with cold meat.

Sweet and Hot!

Mixing sweet things with a bit of spicy heat will make an intriguing flavor combo. Think of all the salsas that mix fruit with jalapeño (or even hotter) peppers—they are wonderful. Try different kinds of fruit sauces, adding a trace of peppery heat each time, until you find several you really like to serve. Experiment with mangos, pineapple, nectarines, apricots, and whatever else is in season. Of course, watch that the sauces you purchase are gluten-free!

Serves 4

½ cup pine nuts, toasted
2 cloves garlic, peeled
4 cups fresh basil leaves, rinsed and packed
½ cup fresh mint leaves, rinsed and packed
1 cup olive oil
1 cup grated Parmesan cheese
Salt and pure black pepper to taste

Appetizers

chapter three

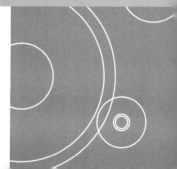

Piquant Artichoke and Spinach Dip

Yields 2 cups

1 10-ounce package frozen chopped spinach, thawed
2 tablespoons olive oil
1 12-ounce jar artichoke hearts, drained and chopped
4 ounces cream cheese
8 ounces GF sour cream
1 teaspoon garlic powder
½ bunch scallions, chopped
2 tablespoons fresh lemon juice
¼ teaspoon freshly grated nutmeg

For perfect party goodies, serve with GF breads and crackers. You can make this in advance and then warm it up at the last minute.

1. Drain the thawed spinach, squeezing it with paper towels until extra liquid is gone.

2. Heat the olive oil and add the spinach; cook until just soft, about 5 minutes.

3. Remove the pan from the heat and add the rest of the ingredients, stirring to mix. Serve warm or cold with celery or GF crackers.

The Artichoke Quandary

Some people absolutely adore artichokes that come in cans or jars; we like fresh or frozen. Cooking artichokes requires a bit more work, but even a busy person can cook ahead. After cooking baby artichokes, you can use them in a number of ways—simply remove the outside leaves.

Spicy Gorgonzola Dip with Red Pepper "Spoons"

This is very flavorful—the more fresh herbs, the better. Try using fresh chives, basil, and oregano.

1. Put all but the raw red peppers into the food processor and blend until smooth. Scrape into a serving bowl.

2. Wash, core, and seed the red bell peppers, and then cut into chunks (these will be your "spoons"). Place the red pepper spoons around the dip.

Exciting and Distinctive— and Healthy—Party Fare

Many of the party appetizers in this chapter are less fattening than plain old cheese and crackers. They are definitely not ho-hum, and many are full of healthful vitamins, minerals, and phytochemicals. Bright red and yellow peppers are an excellent source of vitamin C.

Yields 2 cups

6 ounces gorgonzola cheese, at room temperature
4 ounces GF mayonnaise
4 ounces cream cheese, at room temperature
2 ounces roasted red peppers (jarred is fine)
2 teaspoons fresh chopped herbs (such as oregano, basil, and chives)
Salt, pure black pepper, and Tabasco sauce to taste
4 sweet red bell peppers

Delicate Beef Fan

Serves 6

2 10-ounce cans GF low-salt
  beef stock
1 tablespoon GF soy sauce
4 large eggs
8 ounces heavy or whipping
  cream
2 teaspoons dry sherry
3 cups fresh baby greens
6 leaves fresh sage, for
  garnish

Serve this delightful custard over baby greens with red wine vinaigrette on the side.

1. Bring the beef stock to a boil and let it boil until it is reduced to about two-thirds. Then add the soy sauce.

2. Preheat oven to 325°F.

3. Whisk the eggs, cream, and sherry in a large bowl. When well blended, whisk in the stock.

4. Spray 6 4-ounce custard cups or ramekins with GF nonstick spray. Divide the custard evenly between the cups. Place the cups in a large roasting pan with 2"-high sides. Set in the middle of the oven, and then add boiling water to the pan.

5. Bake the custards until just set, about 30 minutes. Turn the custards out onto a bed of greens. Decorate each with a fresh sage leaf and serve warm.

Light Gorgonzola and Ricotta Torte Appetizer

This is light and delicious. You will find that this works best in a springform pan. Serve warm or at room temperature.

1. Preheat oven to 350°F.

2. Whirl the cheeses, oregano, lemon juice, zest, salt, and pepper in a food processor until very smooth. Place in a bowl and fold in the beaten egg whites.

3. Spray the inside of a 10" springform pan. Add the cheese mixture, and bake for about 30 minutes or until slightly golden.

4. Sprinkle with hazelnuts. Cool slightly and serve in wedges.

The Ties That Bind

Gluten is the glue that holds breads, cakes, and piecrusts together. When you substitute gluten-free flours for gluten-containing flours, you must use eggs or other stabilizers such as guar gum or xanthan gum to hold things together. However, as well as eggs work for some recipes, forget about making gluten-free pasta—you need so much guar gum or xanthan gum that it gets slimy.

Serves 6

16 ounces fresh whole-milk ricotta cheese
4 ounces gorgonzola cheese, crumbled
1 teaspoon fresh oregano, or ¼ teaspoon dried
1 teaspoon fresh lemon juice
1 teaspoon freshly grated lemon zest
Salt and pure black pepper to taste
3 egg whites, beaten stiff
½ cup hazelnuts, chopped and toasted for garnish

Savory Chicken Spread

Makes 3 cups

2 cups cooked white or dark
    chicken
1 stalk celery, coarsely
    chopped
1–2 scallions, white parts
    peeled
2 shallots, peeled
⅔ cup GF mayonnaise (not
    low fat)
1 teaspoon GF curry powder
1 teaspoon GF Dijon mustard
1 teaspoon dried thyme leaves
½ teaspoon celery salt
Salt and freshly ground black
    pepper to taste
½ cup fresh parsley, rinsed
    and chopped

You can use leftover roast chicken or turkey
for an excellent substitution. This works
nicely as a canapé, a stuffing for celery, or a
spread for tea sandwiches.

1. Place all ingredients in a food processor and
whirl until coarsely blended.

2. Scrape into an attractive bowl and chill until
ready to serve. Good with toasted gluten-free
baguette slices, chips, or on lettuce as a first
course. Possible garnishes include chopped
chives, capers, sliced green or black olives, or
baby gherkin pickles.

Hearty Mushrooms Stuffed with Spicy Beef

This recipe is wonderful on a chilly night. You can even increase the portions and serve the mushrooms for lunch with a bowl of soup on the side.

1. To make the filling, place the beef, egg, chili sauce, garlic, onion, spices, and salt in the food processor and mix thoroughly.

2. Carefully remove the stems from the mushrooms and pack them with the filling.

3. Preheat the oven to 325°F. Place the mushrooms in a baking pan and add enough water or white wine to cover the bottom of the pan.

4. Sprinkle with cheese and pine nuts. Bake for 35 minutes.

The Versatile Mushroom

Today, you can get really excellent commercially grown exotic mushrooms. Mushrooms can be called wild only if gathered in the wild. Try baby bellas, which are small portobello mushrooms. Shiitakes are very fine in flavor, and oyster mushrooms are delicious. If you have no budgetary constraints, buy morels or chanterelles.

Serves 4

6 ounces lean ground beef
1 egg
2 tablespoons GF chili sauce
1 teaspoon minced fresh garlic
½ cup chopped red onion
1 inch fresh gingerroot, peeled and minced
⅛ teaspoon ground cinnamon
½ teaspoon dried pure red pepper flakes, or to taste
½ teaspoon freshly ground black pepper
Salt to taste
8 very large fresh mushrooms
Water or white wine (enough to cover bottom of pan)
8 teaspoons freshly grated Parmesan cheese for topping
¼ cup pine nuts, for topping

Devilish Egg-Stuffed Celery

Serves 12

6 eggs, hard-boiled, cooled in water, cracked, and peeled
2 tablespoons GF mayonnaise
6 drops Tabasco sauce
Freshly ground white pepper to taste
1 teaspoon celery salt
1 tablespoon GF Dijon mustard
2 tablespoons chopped onion
1 clove garlic, chopped
Salt to taste
2 tablespoons heavy cream
4 stalks celery, washed and cut into thirds

For garnish: 3 teaspoons GF salmon caviar, 3 teaspoons capers, 3 teaspoons green peppercorns, chopped fresh parsley, hot or sweet Hungarian paprika

This is a different take on deviled eggs—you devil the whole egg. The great thing about hard-boiled eggs is that they can be prepared simply for kids or exquisitely for adults.

1. Place all ingredients except the celery and the garnishes in a food processor and blend until smooth.

2. Spread the mixture in the celery and cover with foil or plastic wrap and chill. Add garnishes just before serving.

An International Flavor

GF chili sauce and GF mayonnaise will add a Russian flavor to the eggs. GF salmon caviar as a garnish will add a Scandinavian touch. Change the amount of heat and the herbs and you will have a different taste sensation. Experiment to find the flavor combinations you like best.

Traditional Chopped Chicken Liver

This can be kosher or not, as the cook decides. When the paté is garnished with GF bacon, it is definitely not kosher.

1. Sauté the onion in 2 tablespoons oil and set aside on paper towels to drain.

2. Sauté the chicken livers in the same pan, adding additional tablespoon of oil if necessary.

3. Either hand chop, grind, or process the livers in a food processor, making sure they are not too fine.

4. Mix the onions, livers, and salt and pepper together and chill.

A Break with Tradition

The recipe here is very basic; it can be changed with the addition of GF bacon, with a tablespoon of brandy, port, or sherry. Crumbled hard-boiled eggs can be sprinkled on top for a different look. However it is served, this is a lovely hors d'oeuvre, fine on GF crackers or thinly sliced GF toast rounds.

Makes 2 cups

1 sweet onion, finely chopped
3 tablespoons olive oil or rendered chicken fat (schmaltz), divided
1 pound fresh chicken livers, trimmed
1 teaspoon kosher salt and freshly ground black pepper to taste

Sicilian Eggplant Rolls

Makes 10 to 15 rolls

1 medium eggplant
   (about 1 pound), peeled
Salt
½ cup olive oil
½ cup rice flour
1 cup ricotta cheese
¼ cup Sicilian olives, pitted
   and chopped
¼ cup Parmesan cheese

Make these in advance and warm them up when your guests come. This also makes a great side dish for dinner.

1. Cut the eggplant in very thin (⅛-inch) slices with a mandolin. Salt the slices and stack them on a plate; let sit under a weight for ½ hour to let the brown juices out.

2. Pat the eggplant slices dry with paper towels.

3. Heat the oil to 300°F. Dip the slices in flour and fry until almost crisp, about 2 minutes per side.

4. Drain the slices and then place a spoonful of the cheese and some chopped olive on the end of each slice. Roll and secure with a tooth-pick.

5. Heat oven to 300°F. Sprinkle the rolls with Parmesan cheese and bake for eight minutes. Serve warm.

Eggplant Makes a Great Wrap

Eggplant can be sliced thinly lengthwise or crosswise and then fried, broiled, or baked. Salting and stacking eggplant slices under a weight will drain off the bitterness that some seem to harbor. Be sure to use a plate with steep sides or a soup bowl under the egg-plant—some give off a lot of juice when salted.

Sweet-Potato Chips

Sweet potatoes are loaded with vitamin A and very delicious when fried and salted. (You can substitute plantains for a taste of the islands.)

Makes about 3 dozen chips

2 large sweet potatoes, peeled
3 cups canola oil
Salt and pure black pepper
  to taste

1. Thin slice the potatoes with a mandoline.

2. Heat the oil in a deep-fat fryer to 375°F.

3. Fry for about 3 to 4 minutes, depending on the thickness of the chips. When the chips are very crisp, remove from the oil and drain.

4. Add salt and pepper. Serve with a GF dip or eat plain.

Mini Quiches

Makes 12

1 package GF piecrust mix
   (made by the Gluten Free
   Pantry)
2 eggs
½ cup grated Jarlsberg
   cheese
¼ cup minced GF prosciutto or
   GF smoked ham
⅔ cup cream
⅛ teaspoon grated nutmeg
2 tablespoons minced fresh
   chives
Freshly ground black pepper
   to taste

A wonderful cocktail party snack. You can vary the ingredients, using Cheddar cheese instead of Jarlsberg and chopped cooked GF bacon instead of GF ham.

1. Preheat the oven to 325°F. Spray a mini-muffin pan with GF nonstick spray and prepare the piecrust mix according to box directions. Roll out thinly. With the rice-floured rim of a juice glass or a 2" biscuit cutter, cut dough into 12 rounds and line the muffin cups with dough.

2. Mix the rest of the ingredients in a food processor.

3. Fill the cups three-quarters full with the cheese mixture.

4. Bake for about 10 minutes, or until the quiches are set. Let rest for 5 minutes. Carefully lift the Mini Quiches from the cups. Serve warm.

Bistro Lentil Salad

This is a favorite in French bistros and Greek tavernas. In either case, the seasonings are only slightly different; in all cases, delicious.

1. Combine the lentils and broth and add water to cover. Add the garlic and cloves. Bring the lentils to a boil and reduce heat to simmer. Cook until tender, about 20 minutes. Drain and place in a large serving bowl. Remove garlic and cloves.

2. Cook bacon, and drain on paper towels.

3. Mix the rest of the ingredients with the lentils and chill for 2 to 3 hours. Just before serving, heat for a few seconds in the microwave. Or serve well chilled with shredded lettuce. Garnish with crisp chopped bacon.

The Lovely Lentil

Lentils are a staple in India, where many people need to be fed on little money. You can become a gourmet on a budget, experimenting with many varieties of lentils. Substitute them for pasta and use them in soups, stews, and salads.

Serves 6

1 (16-ounce) package red lentils or small French ones
2 cups GF chicken broth
Water, as needed
2 cloves garlic, smashed and peeled
2 whole cloves
4 slices GF smoked bacon
½ cup finely chopped sweet red onion
1 sweet red bell pepper, roasted, peeled, and chopped
2 stalks celery, washed and finely chopped
½ cup chopped fresh parsley
2 teaspoons dried oregano
1 teaspoon prepared GF Dijon mustard
2 tablespoons lemon juice
2 tablespoons red wine vinegar
⅔ cup extra-virgin olive oil
Salt and freshly ground pepper to taste

Golden Parmesan Crisps

Makes 12 crisps

2 tablespoons unsalted butter
(more if necessary)
12 heaping tablespoons
coarsely grated fresh
Parmesan cheese
Freshly ground black or
cayenne pepper to taste

It's important to use a block of fresh Parmesan cheese; the bottled stuff won't work as well because it's too fine and too dry. Use the coarse grating blade of a food processor or box grater.

1. Heat the butter in a pan over medium heat until it bubbles.

2. Spoon the cheese by tablespoonfuls onto the butter, pressing down lightly with the back of the spoon to spread.

3. After about 2 minutes, turn and sauté until both sides are lightly golden brown. Add more butter if necessary.

4. Sprinkle with black pepper or cayenne, or both. Serve at once.

Classic Caesar Salad with Gluten-Free Croutons

Caesar salad has become unbelievably popular—it is served with fried calamari, grilled chicken, shrimp, fish, and vegetables.

1. Wash and spin-dry the lettuce; then chop, wrap in a towel, and place in the refrigerator to crisp.

2. Whisk together the egg, egg yolk, lemon juice, garlic, mustard, anchovy paste, and olive oil until very smooth. Add salt and pepper to taste. Add the greens and toss.

3. Sprinkle with Parmesan cheese and croutons, and serve.

Not That Caesar

According to the JNA Institute of Culinary Arts in Philadelphia, Caesar salad was originally created in 1924 by Caesar Cardini, an Italian restaurateur in Tijuana, Mexico. The salad is named after its creator—a chef—not Julius Caesar of the Roman Empire.

Serves 4

1 head romaine lettuce, washed, dried, and chopped into bite-sized pieces
1 whole egg and 1 egg yolk, beaten
Freshly squeezed juice of ½ lemon
2 cloves garlic, minced
1 teaspoon GF English mustard
1 inch GF anchovy paste or 2 canned anchovies, packed in oil, mashed
¾ cup extra-virgin olive oil
Salt and freshly ground black pepper to taste
6 tablespoons freshly grated Parmesan cheese
24 Fresh Gluten-Free Croutons (see page 42)

Fresh Gluten-Free Croutons

Makes 24 croutons

½ cup olive oil
2 cloves garlic, minced or put
   through a garlic press
4 slices GF bread, thickly cut,
   crusts removed
Salt and pure black pepper
   to taste

These can be made in advance and stored in the refrigerator, then crisped up at the last moment. Double the recipe for extras.

1. Preheat the broiler to 350°F.

2. Mix the oil and garlic. Brush both sides of the bread with the garlic oil. Sprinkle with salt and pepper to taste.

3. Cut each slice of bread into 6 cubes, to make 24 cubes. Spray a cookie sheet with GF nonstick spray. Place the cubes on the sheet and broil until well browned on both sides.

4. Put the cookie sheet on the bottom rack of the oven. Turn off the oven and leave the croutons to dry for 20 minutes.

5. Store in an airtight container until ready to use.

For the Love of Garlic

Garlic will give you various degrees of potency depending on how you cut it. Finely minced garlic, or that which has been put through a press, will be the strongest. When garlic is sliced, it is less strong, and when you leave the cloves whole, they are even milder.

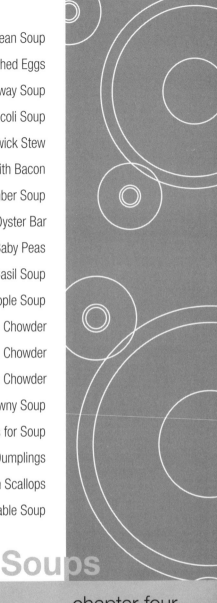

Soups

chapter four

Spicy Mexican Black Bean Soup

Makes about 3 quarts

1 pound ham hocks, split
1 pound black beans, soaked
   in fresh water overnight
2 onions, chopped
4 cloves garlic, minced
2 cups GF beef broth
Juice of 1 fresh lime
1 large (½ pound) Idaho or
   Yukon Gold potato, peeled
   and chopped
2 carrots, peeled and cut up
2 jalapeño peppers, cored,
   seeded, and chopped
1 tablespoon ground cumin
1 tablespoon ground coriander
Salt and freshly ground black
   pepper to taste
½ cup chopped fresh Italian
   flat-leaf parsley or cilantro
1 cup golden rum
GF sour cream and thinly
   sliced lemon or lime to
   garnish

This traditional soup is easy but takes quite a while. It freezes beautifully, so make a lot.

1. Cover the ham hocks with cold water, bring to a boil, cover, and lower heat to simmer. Simmer for 4 hours or overnight. Cover the beans with cold water and soak overnight.

2. Remove the meat from the pot and reserve the cooking liquid. Remove the meat from the bones, discard the skin and bones, and chop the meat. Add the beans to the cooking liquid from the ham.

3. Stir beef broth, lime juice, vegetables, spices, and salt and pepper into the pot with the beans and cooking liquid. Add enough water to make 3½ quarts. Cover and simmer for 5 hours.

4. Stir in parsley or cilantro, taste for seasonings, and add salt and pepper if necessary. Puree the soup in batches and return to the pot to heat. Return the meat to the pot.

5. Either add all of the rum at once and serve, or you can add it to individual bowls of soup. Top each bowl of soup with sour cream and a slice of lemon or lime.

Soaking Beans: The Long and Short of It

Our fast-food culture has moved the packagers of many varieties of dried beans to tell the consumer to boil the beans and then soak them for a short period of time. Sounds like a good idea; however, this method soon separates the bean from its skin and just does not make for a good texture, whether you are leaving the beans whole or pureeing them. If you are short on time, use canned beans.

Onion Soup
with Poached Eggs

When you come in from sledding or skiing, this brunch is about as good as it gets. Everything but the eggs can be made in advance.

1. Fry the bacon until crisp and drain on paper towels; when cool, crumble.

2. Sauté the onions in the olive oil, stir in the flour, and cook for a few minutes, stirring to get rid of the lumps. Add the broth, wine, thyme, and Worcestershire sauce. Cover and simmer over low heat for 1 hour.

3. Just before serving, raise the heat, taste for salt and pepper. Swirl the soup and add the eggs, one at a time. Remove the eggs after 1 minute. Ladle soup and 1 egg each into four warm bowls and garnish with chopped parsley.

Serves 4

4 slices GF bacon
2 Vidalia onions, sliced thin
2 red onions, sliced thin
2 yellow onions, sliced thin
4 tablespoons olive oil or unsalted butter
1 tablespoon chickpea flour
4 cups low-salt GF beef broth
¼ cup dry red wine
1 tablespoon thyme
1 tablespoon GF Worcestershire sauce
Salt and pure black pepper to taste
4 eggs
¼ cup chopped fresh parsley

Carrot, Cauliflower, and Caraway Soup

Serves 4 to 6

1 pound cauliflower florets, rinsed

1 pound carrots, peeled and cut into 1-inch pieces

4 cups GF chicken broth

1 teaspoon caraway seeds

Juice of ½ lemon

1 tablespoon finely grated orange zest

Salt and pure black pepper to taste

1 cup heavy cream

½ cup chopped fresh parsley, for garnish

½ cup snipped fresh chives, for garnish

This simple soup is full of intriguing flavors, delicious as a first course or with a salad alongside for lunch.

1. Boil the cauliflower and carrots in the broth with caraway seeds, lemon juice, orange zest, salt, and pepper.

2. When tender, about 15 to 20 minutes, cool and then puree in food processor or blender until smooth. Taste for salt and pepper, add cream.

3. Reheat but do not boil. Serve, garnished with the herbs.

Thick and Rich Cream of Broccoli Soup

This soup can be served in small cups as a first course, or in bowls as a hearty lunch or supper. Garnish with a few small shrimp floated on the top.

1. Wash, trim, and coarsely chop the broccoli; set aside in a colander to drain.

2. In a large soup pot, heat the oil or butter and add onion and garlic. Sauté until softened. Stir in the cornstarch and liquid ingredients. Mix in the broccoli, nutmeg, juice and rind of lemon, salt, and pepper.

3. Simmer the soup, covered, until the broccoli is tender, about 15 minutes. Remove the lemon rind. Puree in batches. Stir in the cream and ham. Reheat but do not boil. Serve hot.

Adding Depth of Flavor to Soup

Adding GF sausage, GF ham, or GF bacon enriches the flavor of soup. The salt and smoke in the curing process of pork plus the herbs and spices used in sausage also add to the flavor of a soup or stew. Smoked ham hocks are a classical tasty touch in Southern cooking. They are inexpensive and meaty, but the skin and bones must be removed before the soup is served.

Serves 4 to 6

1 pound broccoli
1 tablespoon olive oil or butter
1 large sweet onion, chopped
2 cloves garlic, chopped
2 tablespoons cornstarch dissolved in ⅓ cup cold water
3 cups GF low-salt chicken broth
½ cup dry white wine
¼ teaspoon freshly grated nutmeg
Juice and rind of 1 lemon
Salt and freshly ground pepper to taste
1 cup heavy cream
¾ cup minced GF prosciutto or other GF smoked ham

Old Southern Brunswick Stew

Serves 6

1 chicken (4 to 5 pounds), cut into serving pieces
⅓ cup rice flour
2 tablespoons butter
1 cup water
2 cups chopped tomatoes, fresh or GF canned
1 onion, chopped
1 cup lima beans
1 cup corn kernels
4 whole cloves
1 tablespoon GF Worcestershire sauce
Salt and pure black pepper to taste

Traditionally a Southern dish, it was originally made with local game. Don't remove the cloves—some families consider it good luck to find a clove in their bowl.

1. Dredge the chicken in the rice flour. In a large soup pot, brown chicken in butter, add water, cover, and simmer over low heat for 20 minutes. Remove chicken from the pot; when cool enough to handle, take the meat from the bones. Discard the bones.

2. While the chicken is cooling, stir the tomatoes and vegetables, cloves, and Worcestershire sauce into the pot and cook until tender, another 15 minutes.

3. Return the chicken meat to the pot and simmer for another 5 minutes. Season with salt and pepper. Serve with rice or mashed potatoes on the side.

Kitchen Sink Soup

According to the old wives' tale, when asked, "What's in the soup?" the cooks would say, "Everything but the kitchen sink!" And so it goes today—a frugal cook uses leftover veggies, stews, and whatever is around to add to a soup base. Adding some canned beans and GF broth to a leftover stew can produce a hearty and nourishing main course.

Harvest Corn Chowder with Bacon

Use fresh ears of corn—with their tiny kernels, they are unbelievably sweet and tender. Frozen or canned corn just won't taste the same in this soup.

1. Fry bacon and drain on paper towels; when cool, crumble and set aside, reserving grease in pan. Sauté the onions, potatoes, and pepper in the bacon grease for 10 minutes, stirring often.

2. Add the cornstarch/water mixture, and stirring constantly, ladle in the chicken broth. Bring to a boil. Cover, lower heat, and simmer for 30 minutes.

3. Stir in the rest of the ingredients. Taste, and season with salt and pepper. Do not boil after adding the cream. Serve hot, sprinkling the top with the crumbled bacon.

Serves 6

½ pound GF bacon
2 large sweet onions, chopped finely
2 large Idaho potatoes, peeled and chopped
1 sweet red pepper, cored, seeded, and chopped
3 tablespoons cornstarch mixed with ¼ cup water until smooth
1 quart homemade or canned low-salt GF chicken broth
3 cups fresh corn removed from cob
1 tablespoon GF salsa
1 cup whole milk
1 cup heavy cream
Salt and pure black pepper to taste
¼ teaspoon ground nutmeg
1 bunch fresh parsley, washed, stems removed, chopped

Summer Cucumber Soup

Serves 4

2 English cucumbers, peeled
   and chopped
2 cups buttermilk
1 cup GF sour cream
2 teaspoons salt
Juice of 1 lemon
Rind of ½ lemon
⅔ tablespoon snipped fresh
   dill weed
½ cup snipped fresh chives
   (snipped to ¼ inch)
Freshly ground pepper to taste

This is so refreshing on a hot day. With few ingredients, you can make an elegant and delightful summer soup.

1. Mix all ingredients in a non-reactive ceramic or porcelain bowl. Chill overnight.

2. Serve in chilled bowls.

Oyster Stew à la Grand Central Oyster Bar

Here's a chance to replicate the cooking at New York City's Oyster Bar, a legendary restaurant located in Grand Central Terminal.

1. Mix 2 tablespoons butter, Worcestershire sauce, and clam broth together in a saucepan over medium heat. Whisk in the cornstarch/water mixture. Add the cayenne, oysters, milk, and heavy cream.

2. Heat carefully over a low flame until quite thick, stirring frequently for about 10 minutes. Just before serving, sprinkle with celery salt and paprika, then float a pat of butter on top of each bowl. Serve with GF oyster crackers on the side.

Serves 4

2 tablespoons unsalted butter
2 tablespoons GF Worcester-shire sauce
1 cup bottled or fresh GF clam broth
2 tablespoons cornstarch mixed with 3 tablespoons cold water
⅛ teaspoon cayenne pepper
1 quart shucked oysters, drained
2 cups milk
1 cup heavy cream
Sprinkle of celery salt and paprika
4 pats butter
GF oyster crackers

Fresh Spring Soup with Baby Peas

Serves 4

1 cup chopped spring onions or scallions
2 cloves garlic, smashed
1 bunch sorrel (or 1 bunch watercress)
10 young dandelion greens (small leaves only)
¼ cup olive oil
2 ounces cornstarch
3 cups GF vegetable stock
⅛ teaspoon ground allspice
Zest of ½ lemon, minced
1½ cups fresh baby peas or 1 (10-ounce) package of frozen peas
1 cup heavy cream
Salt and pure black pepper to taste

For a change, mix frozen petit pois (tiny peas) with chopped sugar snaps. Garnish with a few cooked shrimp or a few table-spoons GF smoked ham, finely chopped.

1. Sauté the onions or scallions, the garlic, and the greens in olive oil for 5 minutes, to wilt them.

2. Whisk in the cornstarch and vegetable stock. Stir in the allspice and lemon zest. When smooth, puree in the blender. Return the soup to the pot and add the peas. Cook for 5 to 8 minutes, or until tender.

3. Add the cream, salt, and pepper. Do not boil, but serve hot.

Springtime, Anytime!

You can enjoy spring flavors any time of year, thanks to California herbs and frozen *petit pois*. If you can get spring onions, fine; if not, use scallions.

Fresh Tuscan Tomato and Basil Soup

This taste is so fresh and delightful, you will want to serve it year-round.

1. Make a roux with the butter and cornstarch; cook over medium heat for 5 minutes. Whirl the tomatoes, basil, and oregano in the blender until smooth. Stir the tomatoes into the hot butter mixture.

2. Bring to a boil and add the milk and cream. Heat over low flame and sprinkle with salt and pepper to taste.

Do Not Boil

When a recipe calls for cream, it's important to heat without boiling. If you boil it, you may get curdled soup. If it does get away from you, add a few tablespoons of boiling water and blend until the curds come back together.

Serves 4

4 tablespoons butter
¼ cup cornstarch
2 cups cherry or grape tomatoes
2 cups fresh basil leaves, stems removed
2 tablespoons fresh oregano leaves
1½ cups milk
1 cup cream
Salt and pure black pepper to taste

Yellow Squash and Apple Soup

Serves 4

2 shallots, minced
1 Granny Smith apple, peeled,
    cored, and chopped
2 medium yellow squash,
    washed and chopped
4 tablespoons butter
3 cups fresh orange juice
1 cup apple juice
Juice of 1 fresh lime
¼ teaspoon ground cumin
⅛ teaspoon ground nutmeg
Salt and freshly ground white
    pepper to taste
4 tablespoons GF sour cream
    for garnish

A refreshing summer soup with loads of flavor. Make a lot and serve it the next day to beat the heat.

1. In a large pot, sauté the shallots, apples, and squash in the butter.

2. Add the rest of the ingredients except for the sour cream.

3. Puree the soup, bring to a boil, and serve hot or cold. Garnish with sour cream.

Rhode Island Clam Chowder

This recipe is very traditional. Many cooks now substitute bacon for salt pork, but it's better to make it the traditional way.

1. Scrub the clams and place them in a large pot. Add 2 cups water, cover, and boil until the clams open. Remove them to a large bowl and let cool; reserve the juice. When cool, remove the clams, discard the shells, and chop the clams in a food processor.

2. In a soup pot, fry the salt pork until crisp. Drain on paper towels. Add the vegetables to the pot and sauté until soft, about 10 minutes over medium heat. Blend in the cornstarch and cook for 2 more minutes, stirring.

3. Add the reserved clam juice and the bay leaves, thyme, and celery salt to the pot. Stir in the Worcestershire sauce, clam broth, chopped clams, and salt pork. Cover and simmer for ½ hour. Before serving remove bay leaves. Add black pepper to taste, garnish with chopped fresh parsley, and serve hot.

Is That Clam Alive or Dead?

Never eat a dead clam. Always run them under cold water and scrub vigorously with a brush. To test for life, tap two clams together. You should hear a sharp click, not a hollow thud. If the clam sounds hollow, tap it again, and then, if still hollow-sounding, discard it.

Serves 4

2 dozen cherrystone clams (2 inches across)
3 ounces salt pork, chopped fine
1 large onion, chopped
1 carrot, peeled and chopped
2 stalks celery with tops, chopped fine
2 large Idaho potatoes, peeled and chopped
1 tablespoon cornstarch (more if you like it really thick)
2 bay leaves
1 teaspoon dried thyme
1 teaspoon celery salt
1 tablespoon GF Worcester-shire sauce
3 cups GF clam broth
Freshly ground black pepper to taste
½ cup chopped fresh parsley for garnish

Manhattan
Red Clam Chowder

Serves 6

1 recipe Rhode Island Clam Chowder (see page 55)
1 28-ounce can GF chopped tomatoes with their juice
Parsley, chopped, for garnish

You can transform Rhode Island Clam Chowder to Manhattan with the addition of some tomatoes. This is so easy and good.

1. After you have completed the recipe for Rhode Island Clam Chowder, add the tomatoes.

2. Cover and simmer for 30 minutes.

3. Serve hot. Garnish with chopped parsley.

Tomato or Cream in Your Clam Chowder?

Manhattan clam chowder, made with tomatoes, is a latecomer to the chowder arena. During the eighteenth and nineteenth centuries, tomato-based chowder was banned in New England. In fact, tomatoes were suspect for many years— it was the invention and distribution of catsup in the early twentieth century that brought the tomato into its own in America.

New England
Clam Chowder

With the base for Rhode Island Clam Chowder, you simply add cream and/or milk to transform a clear chowder into a rich and creamy one.

1. Bring the chowder base to a slow boil before adding the milk and cream.

2. Reduce the heat to simmer and cover to let the ingredients marry. After you add the milk and cream, do not boil. If you do, your soup is likely to curdle.

3. Taste and adjust seasonings, if necessary. Garnish with freshly chopped parsley.

Serves 4 to 6

1 recipe Rhode Island Clam
  Chowder (see page 55),
  with an extra tablespoon
  cornstarch added for a
  thicker consistency
1 cup whole milk
1 cup cream
Parsley, chopped, for garnish

Indian Mulligatawny Soup

Serves 4 to 6

1 large sweet onion, such as Vidalia, chopped
4 cloves garlic, chopped
2 tablespoons minced fresh gingerroot
1 hot pepper, serrano or poblano, cored, seeded, and chopped
½ cup unsalted butter
1½ tablespoons GF curry powder, or more to taste
¼ cup rice flour
10 cups GF chicken broth
2 cups red lentils
1 (13-ounce) can pure unsweetened coconut milk
1 teaspoon salt, or to taste
Freshly ground black pepper to taste
6 sprigs fresh coriander leaves for garnish
Lemon slices for garnish

This is a staple in India and best made a day in advance. You may have to thin it out with more water or broth if it gets too thick.

1. Sauté the onions, garlic, ginger, and pepper in the butter over medium heat until soft.

2. Blend in the curry powder and rice flour. Cook for 4 minutes; add the chicken broth and lentils, mixing thoroughly. Simmer, covered, for 1 hour or until the lentils are very tender.

3. Cool and then puree in the blender. Add the coconut milk, salt, and pepper, and reheat. Garnish with coriander sprigs and slices of fresh lemon.

Healthy Soup

The healing qualities of chicken soup plus the healthful properties of Indian herbs and spices make this a very nourishing soup. The name means "pepper water."

Delicious Dumplings for Soup

Dumplings are fun and delicious. They add body to soups and stews.

1. Mix all ingredients together and work into a stiff dough.

2. Drop by the teaspoonful into any soup you are preparing.

3. Let cook for 2 to 3 minutes before serving.

Serves 4

5 tablespoons potato flour
1 teaspoon GF baking powder
1 tablespoon milk
1 egg, beaten
1 teaspoon dried chives or oregano or ⅛ teaspoon nutmeg
½ teaspoon pure ground black pepper

Puffy Potato Dumplings

Serves 4

3 ounces milk or cream

1 teaspoon GF baking powder

½ teaspoon pure ground white or black pepper

½ teaspoon salt

1 whole egg, beaten

1 cup riced or mashed potatoes

2 egg whites, beaten stiff

These give a satisfying finish to a thick soup or rich stew. Riced potatoes work better than mashed for this.

1. Mix the milk, baking powder, pepper, salt, and whole egg into the potatoes.

2. Gently fold in egg whites. Drop by table-spoonfuls on top of stew. Let simmer for 3 to 4 minutes.

3. Run under the broiler until delicately browned.

Shrimp Bisque with Scallops

This is an elegant first course or a delicious lunch. It's very easy to make in advance, adding the cream at the last minute when heating.

1. Sauté the shallots in the butter. Blend in cornstarch and tomato paste. Add broth and bring to a boil. Simmer for 10 minutes.

2. Spoon in the shrimp and scallops. Let cool. Blend in batches until pureed. Return to the pot and add cream. Taste for salt and pepper, adding as necessary.

3. Spoon in the sherry. Garnish with parsley.

Serves 4 to 6

2 minced shallots
2 tablespoons butter
2 tablespoons cornstarch
1 tablespoon GF tomato paste
4 cups bottled GF clam broth
½ pound shrimp, cleaned and deveined
½ pound bay scallops
1 cup heavy cream
Salt and pure black pepper to taste
1 tablespoon dry sherry per bowl of soup
Chopped parsley for garnish

Italian Sausage, Bean, and Vegetable Soup

Serves 4 to 6

1 pound GF Italian sausage, either sweet or hot, cut into 1-inch pieces
1 large red onion, chopped
4 cloves garlic, minced
¼ cup olive oil
1 28-ounce can GF crushed tomatoes with their juice
Bunch escarole, washed, base stems removed, chopped
2 (13-ounce) cans GF beef broth
2 (13-ounce) cans white beans
1 tablespoon dried oregano
1 cup grated Parmesan cheese

There's nothing like a bowl of good soup, especially when you are in a hurry. This one is quite quickly made and will make you feel warm inside.

1. Sauté the sausage, onion, and garlic in the olive oil.

2. When the onion and garlic are soft, add the rest of the ingredients, except the Parmesan cheese.

3. Cover and simmer over very low heat for 30 minutes. Garnish with Parmesan cheese and serve.

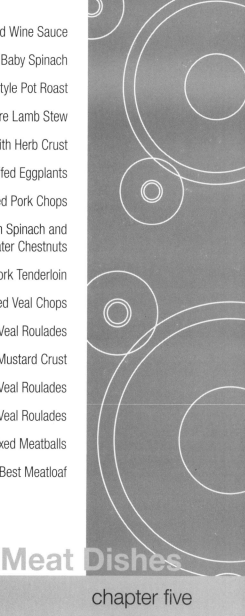

Meat Dishes

chapter five

Stuffed Filet Mignon with Red Wine Sauce

Serves 10 to 12

4 tablespoons unsalted butter
4 cups exotic mushrooms such as criminis, morels, shiitakes, or oysters, brushed off, stems removed, chopped fine
6 shallots, peeled and minced
4 cloves garlic, peeled and minced
1 tablespoon GF Worcestershire sauce
¼ cup chestnut flour, mixed with salt and pure black pepper to taste
½ cup dry red wine, divided
4 sage leaves, torn in small pieces
1 6-pound filet mignon, fat trimmed
½ cup chestnut flour
1 tablespoon coarse salt
1 teaspoon pure black pepper
1 cup GF beef broth
2 tablespoons olive oil

Stuffing a whole filet mignon with mushrooms and garlic will turn it into a luscious feast. Using chestnut flour will add a nutty and delightful flavor.

1. Melt the butter and sauté the mushrooms, shallots, and garlic until the vegetables are soft and the mushrooms are wilted. Add the Worcestershire sauce. Add ¼ cup flour seasoned with salt and pepper and blend; stir in ½ cup red wine and sage. Reduce to about 1½ cups.

2. Preheat oven to 350°F.

3. Make a tunnel down the middle of the filet mignon—use a fat knitting needle or the handle of a blunt knife. Stuff the mushroom mixture into the tube. If there are extra mushrooms, save for the sauce.

4. Coat the outside of the filet with ½ cup chestnut flour, salt, and pepper. Place the remaining ½ cup red wine and beef broth in the bottom of a roasting pan with the filet. Sprinkle with olive oil and roast in oven for 20 minutes per pound.

Drippings Make the Perfect Sauce

Use the drippings for sauce, served on the side. If the pan juices get too reduced, add some boiling water or more beef broth.

Marinated Spicy Beef and Baby Spinach

After you have marinated the beef, the dish takes but a few minutes to cook. Garnish with a few slices of lemon or lime.

1. In a large bowl or glass baking dish, mix together the garlic, 2 tablespoons sugar, salt, pepper flakes, and 2 tablespoons oil. Add the slices of filet mignon, turning to coat. Cover and refrigerate for 2 hours.

2. Mix together the wine, vinegar, 2 teaspoons sugar, and fish sauce; set aside. Heat a nonstick pan over very high heat and add 2 tablespoons oil. Quickly sauté the filets until browned on both sides, about 2 minutes per side. Arrange the meat over a bed of spinach.

3. Add the wine mixture and butter to the pan and deglaze, reducing quickly. Pour over the spinach and meat. Serve with GF soy sauce and chopped scallions on the side and slices of lemon or lime.

Fish Sauce

Fish sauce, available at Asian markets, is an important ingredient in Southeast Asian, Chinese, and Indonesian cuisines.

Serves 4

2 cloves garlic, minced
2 tablespoons sugar
½ teaspoon salt, or to taste
1 teaspoon pure red pepper flakes, or to taste
2 tablespoons canola oil
1½ pounds filet mignon, trimmed and cut into ½-inch slices
¼ cup dry white wine
¼ cup white wine vinegar
2 teaspoons sugar
2 tablespoons GF fish sauce
2 tablespoons canola or peanut oil
4 cups fresh baby spinach, rinsed, spun dry, stems removed
1 tablespoon butter

For garnish: GF soy sauce, chopped scallions, and lemon and lime slices

Gascony-Style Pot Roast

Serves 6

1 4-pound top or bottom
round beef roast
4 cloves garlic, slivered
1 teaspoon salt
1 teaspoon freshly ground
black pepper
Pinch each of cinnamon and
nutmeg
1 slice GF bacon, cut into
pieces
4 shallots, peeled and halved
2 red onions, peeled and
quartered
2 ounces cognac
2 cups red wine
1 cup rich GF beef broth
1 teaspoon thyme
4 whole cloves
¼ cup cornstarch mixed with
⅓ cup cold water until
smooth

This is a traditional holiday dish, often made on Christmas Eve to serve on Christmas Day. Serve with mashed potatoes and winter vegetables.

1. Make several cuts in the meat and put slivers of garlic in each. Rub the roast with salt, pepper, and pinches of cinnamon and nutmeg.

2. Heat the bacon on the bottom of a Dutch oven. Remove the bacon before it gets crisp, and brown the roast. Surround the roast with shallots and onions. Add the cognac, wine, beef broth, thyme, and cloves.

3. Place in a 250°F oven for 5 to 6 hours. When the meat is done, place the roast on a warm platter.

4. Add the cornstarch-and-water mixture to the pan juices and bring to a boil. Slice the roast. Serve the sauce over the pot roast with the vegetables surrounding the meat.

A Hearty, Delectable Pot Roast

Crock-Pots are excellent for cooking a pot roast. Either a top or bottom round is great. Chuck tends to be stringy. Trim the roast well, but do leave a bit of fat on it. You can also marinate a pot roast overnight in red wine and herbs. That will give you a deliciously tender piece of meat.

Thick and Hearty Lancashire Lamb Stew

Make a double recipe and freeze half for another busy day. Cook beans the old-fashioned way or use canned cannellini beans instead.

1. Heat the olive oil in a big, heavy-bottomed stew pot. Dredge the meat with flour, salt, and pepper. Brown the meat, including the bacon. Add the garlic, onions, carrots, and bay leaves.

2. When the vegetables are soft, add the broth, wine, and herbs. Stir in the lemon juice and zest and the Worcestershire sauce.

3. Cover and cook for 3 hours. Pour off the broth and put in the freezer to bring the fat to the top. When the meat is cool enough to handle, remove from the bones.

4. Return the meat and broth to the pot. If too thin, mix 2 tablespoons of cornstarch with 3 tablespoons water and add. Bring to a boil.

5. Stir in the beans. Cover and cook at a simmer for 20 minutes.

Serves 6

¼ cup olive oil
2 pounds lamb stew meat
½ cup potato flour
Salt and pure black pepper to taste
2 slices GF bacon, chopped
4 cloves garlic
2 large onions
2 carrots, peeled and chopped
2 bay leaves
2 cups GF chicken broth
1 cup dry white wine
½ bunch parsley
2 tablespoons dried rosemary
Juice and zest of ½ lemon
2 teaspoons GF Worcestershire sauce
1 1-pound bag great northern beans, soaked overnight and then simmered for 5 hours, or 3 13-ounce cans white beans, drained

Baby Rack of Lamb with Herb Crust

Serves 4 to 6

2 racks of lamb, 1½ to 2
 pounds each, most of the
 fat removed
2 teaspoons salt
Freshly ground black pepper
 to taste
1 cup cornmeal
2 tablespoons dried rosemary
 or 4 tablespoons finely
 chopped fresh
3 tablespoons minced fresh
 parsley
2 tablespoons minced chives
2 tablespoons minced garlic
½ cup olive oil
6 sprigs fresh mint and lemon
 wedges to garnish

This recipe with herbs and cornmeal rather
than white bread crumbs is just delicious.

1. Preheat the broiler to 450°F. Rub the lamb
with salt and pepper. Place on a broiler pan,
bones-side up. Broil for 5 minutes.

2. Turn and continue to broil for another 5
minutes. While the lamb is broiling, mix the
rest of the ingredients together. Press the herb
mixture into the meat and change the setting
from broil to bake. Bake the lamb at 450°F for
another 10 to 12 minutes.

3. Cut into chops and serve.

Mincing Chives

Of course, you can use a knife to mince chives;
however, a pair of sharp kitchen scissors works
faster and better than a knife. The scissors work
well with any number of other ingredients too,
such as scallions, bacon, et cetera. As with any
cutting tool, the sharper, the better—and safer.
Dull tools are dangerous—they can slip off a
tomato, for example—and inefficient.

Greek Lamb-Stuffed Eggplants

You can do most of this in advance, refrigerate, and then put it in the oven for 10 minutes. Serve on beds of lettuce or rice.

1. Fry the whole eggplants in olive oil. When cool enough to handle, make a slit from top to bottom but do not cut through.

2. Over moderate heat, fry the onion, garlic, lamb, salt, pepper, tomato, and herbs. Moisten with lemon juice.

3. Keep stirring to blend and break up the lamb. Set aside to cool for 15 minutes. Place the eggplants on a baking sheet that has been covered with aluminum foil. Spread the eggplants open and fill with lamb stuffing.

4. Preheat oven to 400°F.

5. Bake for 10 minutes. Serve with a dollop of plain yogurt on each eggplant and garnish with mint and chopped tomato.

Lamb Fat

Lamb fat on a chop or roast is strong and must be trimmed away. You can always moisten lamb with GF bacon, olive oil, or butter; just don't cook the fat.

Serves 4 for lunch,
  8 as appetizers

8 small eggplants, about 4 to
  5 inches in length
½ cup olive oil
½ cup minced onion
4 cloves garlic, minced
½ pound lean ground lamb
Salt and pure black pepper
  to taste
½ cup fresh tomato, finely
  chopped
3 tablespoons chopped fresh
  mint
¼ teaspoon ground coriander
Juice of ½ lemon
For garnish: Plain yogurt,
  extra mint leaves, and finely
  chopped tomato

Stuffed Pork Chops

Serves 4

1 tart apple, peeled, cored, and chopped
½ cup chopped onion
1 tablespoon dried rosemary, crumbled, or 2 tablespoons chopped fresh
¼ cup finely chopped Italian flat-leaf parsley
½ cup olive oil
½ cup GF cornbread crumbs
Salt and pure black pepper to taste
4 thick-cut pork rib chops
¼ cup olive oil
4 garlic cloves, chopped
2 onions, chopped
½ cup GF chicken broth
½ cup dry white wine
Zest and juice of ½ lemon
2 ripe pears, peeled, cored, and quartered
2 teaspoons cornstarch mixed with 2 ounces cold water (to thicken the gravy)

Ask the butcher to cut thick rib chops, and to slit a pocket in each. The pears become part of the sauce, and the thickening is optional.

1. Sauté the apple, onion, and herbs in ½ cup olive oil. When softened, add the cornbread crumbs, salt, and pepper. When cool enough to handle, stuff into the chops and secure with toothpicks.

2. Add ¼ cup olive oil to the pan and brown the chops on medium-high. Add the rest of the ingredients, except for the cornstarch-and-water mixture, and cover. Simmer for 40 minutes over very low heat.

3. Place the chops on a warm platter and add the cornstarch-and-water mixture to the gravy in the pan if you want it to be thicker. Add salt and pepper to taste.

Tenderloin of Pork with Spinach and Water Chestnuts

For convenience, use fresh baby spinach, pre-washed and packed in a bag. Serve this dish with rice.

1. Trim the pork and cut into serving pieces. On a sheet of waxed paper, mix together the flour and seasonings. Dredge the pork in the mixture.

2. Sauté the pork in the olive oil for about 6 minutes per side; it should be medium.

3. Add the lemon juice, Worcestershire sauce, spinach, and water chestnuts. Stir to wilt. Sprinkle with more olive oil if the pan is dry.

Buying Pork

You can get "heirloom" or "heritage" pork on the Web. Or you can get pork tenderloin in almost any supermarket. The tenderloin is about the best and most juicy cut available.

Serves 4

2 pork tenderloins, about ¾ pound each
¼ cup potato flour
¼ teaspoon nutmeg
¼ teaspoon ground cloves
Salt and pure black pepper to taste
¼ cup olive oil
2 tablespoons lemon juice
1 teaspoon GF Worcestershire sauce
1 8-ounce bag fresh baby spinach or 1 10-ounce box frozen chopped spinach, thawed
½ cup sliced water chestnuts

Fruit and Corn-Crusted Pork Tenderloin

Serves 4 to 6

6 dried apricots, chopped
½ cup dried cranberries
¼ cup white raisins (sultanas)
1 cup warm water
Juice of ½ lemon
2 pork tenderloins, about
   ¾ pound each
GF Worcestershire sauce
1 cup cornmeal
1 teaspoon salt
Freshly ground black pepper
   to taste
½ cup olive oil

The colorful filling makes this a very pretty presentation. It also is very flavorful.

1. Put the dried fruit in a bowl with the warm water and lemon juice. Let stand until most of the water is absorbed.

2. Preheat oven to 350°F.

3. Make a tunnel through each tenderloin using a fat knitting needle or the handle of a blunt knife. Stuff the fruit into the tunnels.

4. Sprinkle both roasts with Worcestershire. Make a paste with the cornmeal, salt, pepper, and olive oil. Spread it on the pork.

5. Roast for 30 minutes. The crust should be golden brown and the pork pink.

Herb-Stuffed Veal Chops

This recipe calls for thick-cut chops. You can use double rib chops with a pocket for the aromatic herbs and vegetables. These can be grilled or sautéed.

1. Sauté the shallots and herbs in butter. Add salt and pepper.

2. Stuff the chops with herbs. Rub chops with olive oil, salt, and pepper.

3. Using an outdoor grill or broiler, sear the chops over high heat. Then, cut heat to medium and cook for 4 to 5 minutes per side for medium or rare chops. Exact time will depend on the thickness.

Serves 4

½ cup minced shallots
2 tablespoons chopped fresh rosemary
2 teaspoons dried basil or 1 tablespoon chopped fresh basil
½ teaspoon ground coriander
2 tablespoons unsalted butter
1 teaspoon salt
Pure black pepper to taste
4 veal rib chops, 1½ to 2 inches thick, a pocket cut from the outside edge toward the bone in each
¼ cup olive oil
Salt and pure black pepper for the chops

Sausage-Filled Veal Roulades

Serves 4

8 veal scallops, pounded very
  thin with a mallet
⅓ pound sweet GF Italian
  sausage, crumbled
½ cup grated Parmesan
  cheese
1 egg, beaten
½ teaspoon pure black pepper
2 tablespoons unsalted butter
¼ cup GF chicken stock
1 cup light cream

This recipe is a snap to double to serve 8 people.

1. Trim the pounded veal scallops to resemble rectangles. In a bowl, mix the sausage, cheese, egg, and pepper; or, if not of a fine consistency, pulse it in the food processor until it resembles coarse crumbs.

2. Spread the sausage stuffing on the veal and roll up tightly from the wide to the shorter end. Secure with kitchen string.

3. Melt the butter in a pan large enough to hold all of the roulades. Turn the veal until lightly browned. Add the stock and cover. Simmer for 30 minutes.

4. Arrange the roulades on a plate. Deglaze the pan with cream and pour it over the veal. You can add extra cheese, parsley, or watercress to garnish.

Roast Leg of Veal with Mustard Crust

This is a very special occasion entrée. You will probably have to special order the veal from your butcher—try to get one that does not exceed 7 pounds.

1. Preheat oven to 400°F.

2. Make a paste with the butter, mustard, flour, garlic powder, and oregano. Rub the veal with salt and pepper. Cover it with the paste.

3. Place the veal in the oven, and add the vermouth. Roast for 15 minutes or until the crust hardens.

4. Arrange the lemon slices on top of the veal. Baste every 15 minutes. Roast for 15 minutes per pound. Carve and serve with pan juices. (Heavy cream can be added to the pan juices to make more sauce.)

The Versatility of Veal

When you prepare veal chops, scallops, stew, or a roast, you can vary the accompanying vegetables, herbs, and spices. Veal should be very young; old veal is beef. The paler the color, the more mild and tender the meat will be. Cuts from the leg make the scallops.

Serves 10 to 12

½ pound unsalted butter,
    at room temperature
½ cup GF Dijon-style mustard
1 cup rice or potato flour
1 teaspoon garlic powder
2 teaspoons dried oregano
1 7-pound veal leg roast, well
    trimmed
Salt and pure black pepper
1 cup dry (white) vermouth
Lemon slices

French Cheese-Filled Veal Roulades

Serves 4

8 veal scallops, pounded very
  thin with a mallet
6 ounces pepper-flavored
  Boursin cheese
1 teaspoon dried oregano or
  2 teaspoons fresh
1 beaten egg
2 tablespoons butter
½ cup dry white wine
1 cup light cream
¼ cup finely grated Parmesan
  cheese
¼ teaspoon ground nutmeg or
  paprika

Be creative—you can use any number of stuffings. The stuffing of Boursin cheese and oregano is very spicy, a nice counterpoint to the creamy sauce.

1. Trim the pounded veal to resemble rectangles. Combine Boursin cheese, oregano, and egg to make the stuffing. Spread on veal. Roll and tie with kitchen string.

2. Melt butter and lightly brown veal; add wine and cover. Cook for 30 minutes.

3. Put veal on a platter and add cream, Parmesan cheese, and nutmeg to the sauce in pan; heat. Dress and serve.

Pounding Veal

A five-pound barbell works great for pounding the meat. Whether scallops or chops, place between slices of waxed paper and, working from the center to the edges, pound away! The meat will be very tender after this process.

Turkish Veal Roulades

Stuffing the veal with a nice tapenade of olives and parsley is another excellent choice.

1. Trim the pounded veal to resemble rectangles. Lay the veal out flat. Mix the olives, scallions, parsley, olive oil, and lemon juice with the beaten egg.

2. Spread on veal scallops. Roll the veal and tie it. Brown in butter. Add wine, cover, and braise over low heat for 30 minutes. Use wine in pan for sauce.

Serves 4

8 veal scallops, pounded very thin with a mallet
10 pimiento-stuffed green olives, minced
8 black olives (Spanish or Greek), pitted and minced
6 scallions, minced
½ cup minced parsley
2 tablespoons olive oil
Juice of ½ lemon
1 egg, beaten
4 tablespoons butter
½ cup dry white wine

Spicy Mixed Meatballs

Makes 10 to 12 meatballs

1 pound meatloaf mix—
    beef, pork, and veal
2 eggs
2 cloves garlic, minced
1 teaspoon dried oregano
½ teaspoon cinnamon
½ teaspoon fennel seeds
½ cup finely grated Parmesan
    cheese
Salt and pure black pepper
    to taste
2 cups crushed low-salt GF
    potato chips, divided
Light oil, such as canola,
    for frying

Meatballs always have bread as a filler and outside coating. Here, we use ground potato chips. The eggs will hold the balls together, and the ground chips taste wonderful.

1. In a large bowl, mix all ingredients except 1 cup of the chip crumbs and the cooking oil.

2. Place a large sheet of waxed paper on the counter. Sprinkle remaining cup of chip crumbs on it.

3. Form meatballs, roll in crumbs, and fry them in oil until well browned. Drain on paper towels and then either refrigerate, freeze, or serve with the GF marinara sauce of your choice.

Spicy Meatballs

You can add flavor to your meatballs by grinding up some sweet or hot GF Italian sausage and mixing it with the beef. A truly great Italian sausage has aromatics like garlic, and herbs and spices like anise seeds.

The Best Meatloaf

This is classic comfort food. With some mashed potatoes and gravy, your family will love it.

1. Preheat oven to 350°F.

2. In the large bowl of a food processor, whirl all ingredients together.

3. Treat a 9" x 5" bread pan with GF nonstick spray. Pour in the meatloaf mixture.

4. Place a roasting pan in the middle of the oven. Add 1 inch of water. Place the bread pan with the meatloaf in the water. Bake for 1 hour and 20 minutes. For an extra touch, drape 2 slices of GF bacon over the top of the meatloaf.

A Hot Water Bath

Baking your meat loaf in a hot water bath enables it to stay juicy. Processing the ingredients makes a much smoother meatloaf than the coarse stuff that you have to chew for a long time. The water bath is called a bain-marie, and it keeps baked foods soft, creamy, and moist.

Serves 6 to 8

1½ pounds ground beef, either chuck or sirloin
½ cup GF chili sauce
½ cup milk
3 eggs
1 cup GF cornbread crumbs
Salt and pure black pepper to taste
2 garlic cloves, minced
1 small onion, minced
1 teaspoon dried rosemary, crumbled
2 teaspoons Lea and Perrin's steak sauce
½ teaspoon nutmeg

Seafood

chapter six

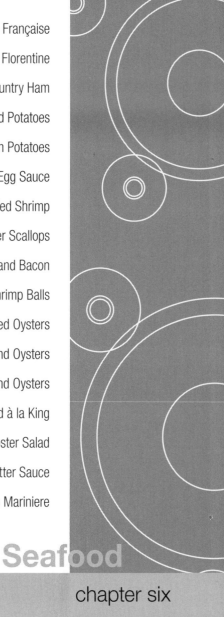

Sole Française

Serves 4

4 5-ounce filets of gray or
    Dover sole
1 egg
Juice of ½ lemon plus
    2 teaspoons lemon juice
    for the sauce
1 cup rice flour
1 teaspoon salt
1 teaspoon pure white pepper
    or to taste
½ cup olive oil
2 tablespoons unsalted butter
2 ounces dry white wine
2 tablespoons capers
½ cup chopped parsley,
    for garnish

Although classic recipes for this fine dish call for all-purpose flour, it is much lighter when you use rice flour. You can substitute flounder for sole.

1. Rinse sole and set on paper towels to dry.

2. Whisk the egg and juice of ½ lemon together.

3. Mix the flour, salt, and pepper on a piece of waxed paper. Heat the olive oil in a nonstick pan over medium-high heat. Dip the pieces of sole in the egg mixture, then in the flour.

4. Sauté the sole until lightly browned, about 3 minutes per side. Don't overcook or it will fall apart. Place on a warm platter.

5. Mix the butter, wine, and capers in the pan used for the fish. Stirring constantly, bring to a boil, then pour over the fish. Sprinkle with parsley and serve.

Buying Fresh Fish

No matter what the sauce, if a fish is not absolutely fresh, it will taste awful. When you buy fish, it should gleam—the eyes should be very bright and shiny, not glazed, and the scales should be silvery and glistening. But the acid test is to smell it. If it smells anything but fresh, don't buy it. It also helps to make friends with the fishmonger. Ask him questions like, "When did this come in?" "What came in this morning?" and "May I smell that?"

Sole Florentine

Sole is an adaptable fish; mild and sweet, it goes with many different flavors. Frozen spinach works fine for this.

1. Melt the butter over medium heat, and sauté the shallot until softened, about 5 minutes. Blend in the cornstarch, cooking until smooth.

2. Add the spinach, cream, and nutmeg. Cook and stir until thickened. Pour into a baking dish treated with GF nonstick spray and set aside.

3. Dip the pieces of sole in beaten egg. Then, on a sheet of waxed paper, mix the flour, salt, and pepper. Dredge the sole in the flour mixture.

4. Sauté the sole in the olive oil until lightly browned. Arrange over the spinach. Sprinkle with cheese. Run under the broiler until very brown and hot, about 3 minutes.

Serves 4

3 tablespoons unsalted butter
1 shallot, minced
3 tablespoons cornstarch
2 10-ounce packages frozen chopped spinach, thawed, moisture squeezed out
⅔ cup heavy cream
¼ teaspoon nutmeg
4 sole filets, rinsed and dried on paper towels
1 egg, well beaten
½ cup rice or potato flour
Salt and pure black pepper to taste
⅔ cup olive oil
¼ cup Parmesan cheese

Maryland-Style Crab Cakes with Country Ham

Makes 8 crab cakes

½ cup GF mayonnaise
2 eggs
1 teaspoon GF Dijon-style mustard
1 teaspoon GF Worcestershire sauce
Salt and 1 teaspoon pure red pepper flakes, or to taste
1 tablespoon fresh lemon juice
1 cup GF cornbread crumbs, divided
1¼ pounds lump blue crab-meat (not imitation)
Oil for frying
Lemon wedges to garnish

The addition of GF country ham balances the sweetness of the crabmeat and gives the whole thing a great lift.

1. In a large bowl, mix the mayonnaise, eggs, mustard, Worcestershire sauce, salt, pepper flakes, and lemon juice. Stir until well mixed.

2. Add half the cornbread crumbs and gently toss in the crabmeat. Form 8 cakes and coat with more cornbread crumbs.

3. Over medium heat, bring the oil to 300°F. Fry the cakes, turning after five minutes, until golden brown. Serve with lemon wedges.

Topping Off Crab Cakes

Some cooks add finely chopped onion to their crab cake mixture. Others use chives. You can also add finely chopped parsley. Some like their crab cakes with GF tartar sauce, others with GF cocktail sauce.

Marseilles Whipped Codfish and Potatoes

This is a dish that a tired Frenchman will make at the end of the week. You can use either salt cod or fresh cod.

1. Soak the codfish overnight in cold water to cover. Change water once or twice.

2. Boil the potatoes in their skins until a knife slides into the flesh easily. The timing varies by the size of the potato.

3. Using a long-handled fork, spear the boiled potatoes and peel them. Put the potatoes through a ricer and into a bowl. Whisk in the olive oil and the milk or cream, then add salt and pepper and keep warm.

4. Steam the cod, salted or fresh, about 15 minutes, until very tender. Make sure there are no bones.

5. Whirl the cod in a food processor until smooth.

6. Fold the cod into the riced potatoes and mixture of parsley and chives.

7. Blend with a fork until fluffy. Serve hot.

Serves 4

2 cups salt codfish, or
 1¼ pounds fresh codfish
3 large or 4 medium potatoes,
 about 2 pounds
2 tablespoons olive oil
½ cup rich milk or light cream,
 use more or less depending
 on the consistency of the
 potatoes
Salt and pure black pepper
 to taste
½ cup each chopped chives
 and parsley

Codfish Broiled on a Bed of Paper-Thin Potatoes

Serves 4

2 pounds of Idaho or Yukon
    Gold potatoes, peeled and
    sliced paper thin
¼ cup olive oil
2 tablespoons butter, melted
Salt and pure black pepper
    to taste
4 cod filets or steaks, about
    5 ounces each
Salt, pure black pepper, and
    butter for the fish
Chopped parsley and lemon
    wedges to garnish

Cod is one of the world's most beloved and versatile fish. It can be baked, broiled, steamed, poached, salted, or cooked with milk in a stew.

1. Preheat oven to 400°F.

2. In a baking pan that has been treated with GF nonstick spray, toss the thinly sliced potatoes with oil and melted butter, salt, and pepper.

3. Bake the potatoes for 40 minutes or until the top is brown and crisp and the inside soft.

4. When the potatoes are done, lay the fish on top, sprinkle with salt and pepper, dot with butter, and reheat the oven to broil.

5. Broil until the fish is done—8 to 10 minutes, depending on the thickness of the fish. If the potatoes start to burn, move the pan to a lower shelf in the oven.

6. Sprinkle with chopped parsley and serve with lemon wedges.

Crabmeat

There is a lot of real crab and fake crabmeat around. (Imitation fish products are not always gluten-free!) The very best is Maryland blue crab, in lumps or flakes; it's also the most expensive, running up to $15 a pound. Fake crab, or surimi, is made from fish that has been cooked with the water and juices from crabmeat; it is cheap. Blue crabs are rounded and squat, unlike the gigantic, spider-like legs of Alaska king crab, or the finger-like clusters of snow crab. There's nothing like a good fresh crab, whether from Alaska or Maryland.

Baccala (Salt Cod) in Thick and Creamy Egg Sauce

This is a very old-fashioned Easter-morning dish. Served over rice or cornbread with hard-boiled eggs in the sauce, it's very satisfying.

1. Drain the baccala and cut it into bite-sized pieces. Quickly sauté it in a pan with the olive oil; set aside.

2. Sauté the onion in butter over medium heat for 6 to 8 minutes. Blend in the cornstarch and dry mustard. Cook for another few minutes and slowly, whisking constantly, blend in the milk. Add the parsley, nutmeg, pepper, and chopped egg.

3. Heat, stirring, until very thick. Stir in the cod and keep stirring until very hot. Sprinkle with pickle and serve over cornbread or rice.

Salt Cod

Having come from dire necessity, salted fish, which would keep during the winter when fishing for fresh fish was impossible, it was looked down on for a time. Now it's viewed with nostalgia, as traditional as any family's food history. Most European countries' cuisines have recipes for salt cod.

Serves 4 to 6

1 pound salt cod, skinless, soaked in cold water for 24 hours, water changed 3 times
2 tablespoons olive oil
¼ cup minced sweet onion
2 tablespoons butter
2 tablespoons cornstarch
½ teaspoon GF dry mustard
1½ cups milk
¼ cup finely chopped parsley
¼ teaspoon nutmeg
Pure black pepper to taste
2 hard-boiled eggs, chopped
2 GF sour pickles, finely chopped
8 to 10 thin slices GF cornbread, or 4 cups cooked rice

Crispy Beer-Battered Fried Shrimp

Serves 4

½ cup corn flour
¼ teaspoon salt
1 tablespoon butter, melted
1 whole egg
½ cup flat buckwheat GF beer
1 egg white, beaten stiff
1¼ pounds shrimp, peeled and
   deveined
¼ cup golden rum
2 tablespoons GF soy sauce
Light oil such as canola, for
   frying

You can do everything in advance but fry the shrimp. Beer batter is delicious and can be used with other seafood as well as with chicken.

1. Make the batter in advance by mixing together the first five ingredients. Let stand for an hour.

2. Marinate the cleaned shrimp in rum and soy sauce for 20 minutes, covered, in the refrigerator.

3. Bring the oil for frying to 375°F. Add the final egg white to the batter. Dip the shrimp in the batter a few times to coat. Gently lower a few shrimp at a time into the oil. Fry for about 4 minutes, or until well browned. Drain on paper towels and serve.

Golden Sautéed
Diver Scallops

This recipe calls for caramelizing the scallops. Now, that's absolutely terrific. And it tastes wonderful. You'll find lots of excuses to serve these.

1. On a sheet of waxed paper, mix the flour, sugar, salt, and pepper. Roll the scallops in the flour mixture.

2. Heat the butter and oil over medium-high heat. Add the scallops and watch them—they will brown quickly. Cook for 2 to 3 minutes per side. Serve with any of your favorite sauces.

Serves 4

½ cup corn flour
2 tablespoons white sugar
1 teaspoon salt
½ teaspoon pure white pepper
1½ pounds large diver scallops, each about 2 inches across
2 tablespoons unsalted butter
2 tablespoons olive oil

Savory Shark and Bacon

Serves 4

2 tablespoons GF chili sauce
1 tablespoon concentrated
    orange juice
1 tablespoon GF Worcester-
    shire sauce
Juice of ½ lemon
1 teaspoon Tabasco sauce, or
    to taste
1¼ pounds boneless shark
    steak, cut into serving
    pieces
Salt and pure black pepper
    to taste
4 strips GF bacon

Shark is a melt-in-your-mouth kind of fish—and it really deserves to be cooked more often. It is sweet and tender.

1. Preheat the broiler to 450°F. Mix the chili sauce, orange juice, Worcestershire sauce, lemon juice, and Tabasco sauce in a small bowl.

2. Rinse and pat the shark steaks dry. Sprinkle with salt and pepper. Paint them with the sauce mixture.

3. Place steaks on a broiler pan that you have treated with GF nonstick spray. Arrange the bacon on top of the shark and broil for 3 minutes. Turn the bacon and broil for 2 more minutes. Turn off the broiler and close the door to let the shark cook through, about 6 minutes.

Chinese Shrimp Balls

Serve with GF hot mustard or any other GF Asian sauce. For a variation, serve with GF tartar sauce.

1. Place the ingredients, except the cooking oil, in the food processor. Pulse, and scrape the sides often.

2. Heat the oil to 360°F. Carefully drop balls by the teaspoonful into the oil. When golden, after about 3 to 4 minutes, place them on a serving platter lined with paper towels or napkins to drain. Serve and enjoy.

Using Fresh Shrimp

Never use precooked shrimp for cooking. It will be rubbery and tough. Cooked shrimp is pink; raw shrimp is grayish or white. It may be a bit of trouble to peel and clean shrimp, but it's well worth it to get the succulent flavor of good fresh shrimp.

Serves 8 to 10 as an appetizer

1 pound raw shrimp, peeled and deveined
1 egg
1 tablespoon dry sherry
2 teaspoons GF soy sauce
1 teaspoon sugar
1 tablespoon cornstarch
1 cup lean ground pork
2 scallions, chopped
3 cups oil for frying

Southern Fried Oysters

Serves 4

1 quart shucked oysters
½ cup corn flour
1 cup cornmeal
1 teaspoon GF baking powder
¼ teaspoon nutmeg
½ teaspoon salt or to taste
Freshly ground black pepper
   to taste
2 beaten eggs
Oil for deep frying

These are so crunchy on the outside and succulent on the inside, you will probably have to make an extra batch. Serve with any of the sauces in this chapter or just a squeeze of lemon juice.

1. Place the oysters in a colander to drain. Thoroughly mix the flour, cornmeal, baking powder, nutmeg, salt, and pepper.

2. Dip the oysters in the egg and then in the flour-and-cornmeal mixture. Bring oil in a pot to 375°F and fry for about 3 to 4 minutes or until browned.

3. Remove with a slotted spoon. Drain on paper towels.

Seafood Loves to Be Saucy

Even the tastiest of mollusks and crustaceans love to be dipped or bathed in sauces, and there are a variety of options and substitutions. Any citrus can be substituted for just about any other, for example, limes for lemons, grapefruit for orange, and you can blend them together for intriguing outcomes using your own original flair for flavors. Throw in some ginger, GF curry powder, or GF mustard and you'll add another layer of flavor.

Spicy Dipping Sauce for Shrimp and Oysters

A good dipping sauce has dozens of uses. Make in advance and store in the refrigerator.

Place all ingredients in the blender and whirl until well blended. Serve.

Makes 1½ cups

1 cup GF chili sauce
1 teaspoon orange bitters
2 teaspoons lemon juice
1 teaspoon grated horseradish
or to taste
1 teaspoon minced fresh
gingerroot
1 teaspoon brown sugar, or
to taste
1 teaspoon cider vinegar
½ teaspoon garlic powder
Salt and pure black pepper
to taste

Citrus Dipping Sauce for Shrimp and Oysters

Makes 1½ cups

½ cup marmalade
¼ cup GF soy sauce
¾ cup fresh orange juice
1 teaspoon GF Dijon mustard
Juice of ½ lime
Juice of ½ lemon
1 inch ginger root, peeled and
   minced
Salt and pure black pepper
   to taste

One of the best things about this sauce is its versatility. You can use it with fried scallops, cold seafood, or chicken.

Place all ingredients in a saucepan and boil ntil well blended. Cool and store in the refrigerator.

Seafood à la King

You can make the sauce the day before and add the seafood at the last minute. Serve with rice or stuffed into crepes.

1. Sauté the shallots in the butter over moderate heat for 5 minutes. Add the mushrooms and pearl onions. Stir, cooking for a few more minutes.

2. Mix the cornstarch with cold water and add to the pan, stirring to blend. Blend in the tomato paste and brandy. Warm the cream slightly, then stir it into the sauce in the pan. (You can prepare this dish in advance up to this point. Store in the refrigerator until ready to serve.)

3. Reheat the sauce but do not boil. Taste for salt and pepper and add the seafood. When the shrimp turns pink, the dish is done. Garnish with caviar and serve.

Long Live the King!

This dish was created at the Brighton Beach Hotel on Long Island, New York, by Chef George Greenwald, for his boss, E. Clarke King, II. It became very popular when Campbell's came out with canned cream of mushroom soup, which could be substituted as a base.

Serves 4

½ cup shallots, minced
¼ cup unsalted butter
20 small white mushrooms, cut in half
20 pearl onions, fresh or frozen, cut in half
2 tablespoons cornstarch
2 ounces cold water
1 tablespoon GF tomato paste
2 tablespoons brandy
1½ cups cream
Salt and pure black pepper to taste
½ pound shrimp, cleaned and deveined
½ pound bay scallops
2 tablespoons GF red salmon caviar for garnish

Shrimp and Lobster Salad

Serves 4

1 cup GF mayonnaise
1 teaspoon GF Dijon mustard
Juice of ½ lime and 1 teaspoon zest
1 teaspoon GF soy sauce
1 tablespoon GF chili sauce
1 teaspoon minced garlic
Salt and pure black pepper
  to taste
Meat of 1 small (1½ pound)
  lobster, cooked
½ pound cleaned and cooked
  shrimp
¼ cup mixed, snipped fresh
  dill weed, and chopped
  fresh parsley
1 tablespoon capers
4 beds of shredded lettuce

Try using different citrus fruits and mixing in different vegetables. Use almonds instead of peanuts. And if you like cilantro, use that instead of parsley.

1. Mix together the mayonnaise, mustard, lime juice and zest, soy sauce, chili sauce, minced garlic, and salt and pepper.

2. Just before serving, mix the sauce with the seafood. Garnish with snipped fresh dill weed and chopped parsley, sprinkle with capers, and serve over a bed of lettuce.

Capers

These tiny berries are pickled in brine or packed in salt. The islands of the Mediterranean are lush with the bushes that produce them and they are used in profusion in many fish, meat, and salad dishes. The French love them, as do the Italians, Greeks, Sardinians, and Maltese. Try some in a butter sauce over a piece of fresh striped bass and you'll understand their popularity.

Poached Monkfish in Caper Butter Sauce

Monkfish is a mild, sweet fish that is wonderful cooked in many ways. It is delicious poached, broiled, or baked.

1. Dredge the fish in flour, then sauté over medium heat in olive oil. Turn after 4 minutes.

2. Add the wine, broth, butter, and capers. Simmer (poach) for about 8 minutes, or until the fish is cooked through. Place fish on a warm plate, reduce sauce to half, and pour over fish.

3. Sprinkle with salt, pepper, and paprika. Serve with lemon wedges.

Monkfish—Poor Man's Lobster

Oddly enough, monkfish was once considered a throwaway fish! It has a slightly hooded flange around its head, like a monk's cowl. It is delicious poached, broiled, or baked. It loves various sauces. The only thing to remember is not to overcook it. Monkfish, when poached in clam juice, water, or white wine, puffs, growing lighter and fluffier. Then all you have to do is add lemon and butter, and it's very much like lobster.

Serves 4

1½ pounds monkfish, cut in 4 serving pieces
½ cup potato flour
2 tablespoons olive oil
¼ cup dry white wine
¼ cup GF chicken broth
1 tablespoon butter
2 tablespoons capers
Salt and pure black pepper to taste
Paprika and lemon wedges for garnish

Mussels Mariniere

Serves 4

½ cup finely chopped onion
2 tablespoons butter
2 tablespoons cornstarch
1 cup dry white wine
½ cup celery tops, chopped
3 to 4 pounds mussels,
  scrubbed and tapped
1 cup heavy cream
Salt and pure black pepper
  to taste
Juice of ½ a lemon
½ cup fresh Italian flat-leaf
  parsley, rinsed and
  chopped

This is a thick, creamy stew. It's absolutely delicious and perfectly quick and simple to make.

1. Sauté the onion in the butter until soft. Work in the cornstarch. Whisk in the white wine and add the celery tops. Mix and bring to a boil.

2. Pour in the prepared mussels. Cover and continue to boil. After two minutes, stir to bring the bottom ones up.

3. Have a large serving bowl on the side of the pot. Remove mussels as they open.

4. When all of the mussels are open and removed from the pot, reduce heat and add the cream. Heat but do not boil. Add salt and pepper to taste.

5. Pour sauce over the mussels; sprinkle with lemon juice and parsley. Serve in warm bowls, with a big bowl for the shells.

Check Your Mussels

You must be sure that your mussels are alive. This means they are shut tightly and when you tap two together, you get a sharp click, not a hollow thump. Often, they will be slightly open but close when tapped—that's fine. Just don't use any that are cracked, open, or hollow-sounding. The same is true for clams. Always scrub clams and mussels with a stiff brush under cold running water.

Poultry

chapter seven

Crispy Potato-Crusted Chicken

Serves 4

12 ounces GF potato chips
4 boneless, skinless chicken breasts
⅔ cup GF sour cream
1 teaspoon freshly ground black pepper
2 tablespoons snipped fresh chives
1 teaspoon dried thyme

When you use this crust on your baked chicken, you'll find it's really crispy and crunchy. Don't add salt, as potato chips are already salty.

1. In a food processor, chop up potato chips until you have 1 cup of crumbs. Mix in peppers, chives, and thyme.

2. Rinse the chicken, dry on paper towels, and lay it in a baking dish that you have prepared with GF nonstick spray.

3. Preheat the oven to 350°F. Spread the chicken with sour cream, sprinkle with the potato-chip mixture, and bake for 25 minutes or until brown and crispy.

Sporting Chicken Tenders

Chicken tenders are the strip along the breast that earns the name "tender." These make a great snack when you have a crowd.

1. Rinse the chicken and dry on paper towels, then lay out two sheets of waxed paper. Mix together the potato flour, salt, pepper, and baking powder and spread it on one sheet.

2. Spread the crumbs on the other piece of waxed paper. Beat the egg and milk together. Dredge the tenders in the potato flour mixture, then dip them into the egg mixture, and finally coat them in the crumbs.

3. In a heavy-bottomed frying pan, heat ½ inch of oil to 365°F and fry the chicken tenders until golden, about 3 to 4 minutes. Drain on paper towels.

Serves 4 to 6

1 pound chicken tenders, cut into bite-sized pieces
1 cup potato flour
1 teaspoon salt
Pure red pepper flakes to taste
1 teaspoon GF baking powder
1 cup fine GF cornbread crumbs
1 well-beaten egg
2 tablespoons milk
Cooking oil as needed

Classic Southern Fried Chicken

Serves 4

1 chicken, cut into 8 pieces
   (drumsticks, thighs, breasts,
   and wings)
1 cup buttermilk
1½ cups corn flour
1 teaspoon salt (or to taste)
1 teaspoon pure black pepper
   (or to taste)
1 teaspoon GF baking powder
1 egg, beaten
½ cup GF buckwheat beer
1½ cups cornmeal
Vegetable oil for frying

A great fried chicken is perfectly delicious. It's wonderful picnic fare and fabulous when you are giving a sports-on-TV party.

1. Rinse the chicken pieces and dry on paper towels, then place in a resealable plastic bag with the buttermilk and marinate for 2 to 3 hours.

2. In a large paper bag, mix together the corn flour, salt, pepper, and baking powder. Add the chicken pieces to the corn flour mixture one at a time, then close the bag and shake until the chicken is well coated.

3. Whisk the egg and beer together. Spread the cornmeal on a large piece of waxed paper. Dip the chicken in the beaten egg/beer mixture, then roll in the cornmeal, pressing it all together.

4. Bring 1 inch of oil to 365°F in a fryer, or ½ inch of oil in a frying pan. Fry the chicken for 20 to 25 minutes; turn every 4 or 5 minutes. Watch the chicken carefully to make sure that it doesn't burn.

Frying with Corn Flour

When you use corn flour or cornmeal for frying, you can mix it with either rice flour or potato flour for good results. For a light, tempura-like crust, try cornstarch mixed with water and egg as a coating. Gluten-free cooking does require a whole new chemistry.

Old-Fashioned Chicken Cacciatore with Spaghetti Squash

You can vary this dish by adding fresh mint, red vermouth rather than red wine, capers, and lemon zest.

1. Dredge the chicken in the flour, salt, pepper, and oregano. Heat the oil and butter together until butter melts. Sauté chicken in the oil-and-butter mixture. Add the onion, garlic, rosemary, and mushrooms. Sauté for 5 minutes.

2. Add the marinara sauce or tomatoes and red wine. Cover and simmer over very low heat for 1 hour. Remove cover, place chicken on a platter, and continue to simmer sauce until reduced by half.

3. Spoon sauce over the chicken and sprinkle with cheese and fresh parsley.

Serves 4 to 6

1 3½-pound chicken, cut into 8 pieces
1 cup potato or corn flour
Salt and pure black pepper to taste
1 teaspoon oregano, crumbled
¼ cup olive oil
1 teaspoon butter
1 onion, peeled and diced
2 to 3 cloves garlic, peeled and minced
2 tablespoons fresh rosemary
2 cups mushrooms, brushed off and chopped
1 16-ounce jar GF marinara sauce or 16 ounces GF canned tomatoes
4 ounces dry red table wine or to taste
½ cup Parmesan cheese
1 bunch fresh parsley, chopped, for garnish

Smooth Chicken and Chicken Liver Paté

Serves 6 to 8

2 tablespoons sweet butter
1 tablespoon olive oil
½ pound chicken livers, rinsed and dried
½ pound boneless, skinless chicken breasts, cut into small pieces
2 tablespoons tapioca flour or cornstarch
Salt and freshly ground white or pink pepper to taste
1 clove garlic, peeled and minced
¼ cup finely chopped sweet onion
¼ cup brandy
3 large eggs
½ cup heavy cream
2 tablespoons tiny capers
2 slices GF bacon, diced

This makes great sandwiches on GF toast with pickles on the side. Or you can serve it with poached eggs for brunch.

1. Heat the butter and oil in a large frying pan. Dredge the livers and chicken in flour, salt, and pepper. Sauté for 10 minutes, turning constantly. Place in a food processor. Blend to a puree.

2. Add the garlic and onion to the pan and cook for just a few minutes. Scrape the garlic and onions into the food processor.

3. Deglaze the pan with the brandy, being sure to get up all of the browned bits sticking to the bottom of the pan. Pour into the processor. Break eggs and drop into the processor.

4. Pour in the cream at the last minute, and as soon as mixed, turn off the processor. Prepare a pan with GF nonstick spray, and pour the mixture into it. Dot the top with capers and bacon.

5. Preheat oven to 325°F.

6. Place the pan in a larger pan half filled with hot water. Bake for 40 minutes. Cool and slice.

Indian-Style Chicken with Lentils

In countries with huge populations, it's both wise and popular to stretch meat, fish, and seafood with all kinds of legumes.

1. Place the lentils and water in a saucepan. Bring to a boil, reduce heat, and simmer.

2. Just before the lentils are cooked (when barely tender, after about 25 minutes), add the salt and pepper, garlic, onion, lemon juice, cumin, and parsley.

3. Toss the chicken with the yogurt, curry powder, salt, and Tabasco. Place on aluminum foil and broil for 5 minutes per side.

4. Mix the chicken into the lentils and serve with rice.

Serves 4 to 6

1 cup lentils
3 cups water
Salt and pure red pepper flakes to taste
2 cloves garlic, peeled and minced
1 onion, peeled and finely minced
2 tablespoons lemon juice
1 teaspoon cumin
½ cup chopped fresh parsley
1 pound boneless, skinless chicken breasts, cut into bite-sized pieces
1 cup plain yogurt
1 tablespoon GF curry powder
Salt and Tabasco sauce to taste

Family-Style Turkey Loaf

Serves 4 to 6

1 pound mixed ground turkey
1 cup ground plain popcorn or
   GF cornbread crumbs
⅔ cup milk
¼ cup GF chili sauce
3 eggs
1 teaspoon thyme
½ cup chopped onion
Salt and pure black pepper
   to taste
¼ teaspoon nutmeg
2 strips GF bacon

This can be served with rice or mashed potatoes on the side. It can be adapted in many ways to suit the family's tastes, from mild to spicy.

1. Preheat oven to 350°F.

2. Put all but the bacon into your food processor and whirl until well blended.

3. Pour into a 9" x 5" bread pan and put that pan into a much larger one (such as an 11" x 13" pan). Place in the oven and add boiling water to the larger pan. Cut the bacon in halves and arrange across the top of the loaf. Bake for 1 hour.

4. Serve with mashed potatoes. For a more grown-up flavor, add 2 ounces of brandy.

Elegant Duckling and Fruit-Filled Corn Crepes

This would be a delicious dinner or lunch served over baby spinach or fresh salad greens. The sweetness of the duck works with the fruit—a marriage made in heaven.

1. Mix the chicken broth and the cornstarch and set aside.

2. Dredge the duck breasts in corn flour and sauté them in butter over medium heat. Add the salt and pepper and the chicken broth/cornstarch mixture to the pan, stirring to make a sauce.

3. Add the soaked fruit, celery tops, onions, rosemary and apple brandy. Cover and cook for 20 minutes over low heat.

4. Preheat oven to 350°F.

5. Cool and remove the duck from the pan. Cut it into small pieces and shred. Return the duck to the sauce. Divide the sauce between the 8 crepes. Roll the crepes, place them seam-side down in a greased baking dish, and drizzle with melted butter or olive oil. Heat them in the oven for 10 to 15 minutes. Serve over greens or sautéed spinach.

Serves 4

½ cup GF chicken broth
1 tablespoon cornstarch
⅔ pound boneless, skinless duck breasts
½ cup corn flour
3 tablespoons unsalted butter
Salt and 2 teaspoons freshly ground black pepper
½ cup dried cranberries soaked in ⅔ cup apple juice or wine
¼ cup dried cherries soaked in ½ cup orange juice
¼ cup chopped celery tops
24 pearl onions (frozen is fine)
½ cup apple brandy (such as Calvados)
1 tablespoon rosemary leaves, dried and crumbled
8 large Corn Crepes (see page 11)
2 tablespoons butter, melted, or olive oil

The Best Roasted Turkey

Serves 15

1 10-pound turkey
¼ pound butter, softened
1 teaspoon dried thyme
½ cup fresh Italian flat-leaf
    parsley, rinsed and minced
Salt to taste and 1 teaspoon
    pure black pepper
Giblets, including wing tips
    and neck
½ cup dry white wine
2 bay leaves
1 recipe Stuffing for Roasted
    Turkey (see page 109)
4 strips GF bacon for bottom
    of roasting pan
2 teaspoons cornstarch
¼ cup water

For the sweetest, juiciest bird, try to find a turkey that is between 9 and 12 pounds. Make extra gravy by adding a can of GF chicken broth to the basting liquid.

1. Rinse the turkey in cold water and pat dry. Mix the butter, herbs, salt, and pepper thoroughly. Tease it under the skin of the breast, working it into the thighs. Be careful not to tear the skin.

2. Place the giblets and wing tips in a saucepan with the wine and water to cover. Add the bay leaves. Cook for 2 hours, or while the turkey is cooking. Add extra water if the broth gets dry.

3. Stuff the turkey and skewer the legs together. Close the neck cavity with a skewer. Preheat the oven to 325°F.

4. Place the bacon on the bottom of the roasting pan and start the turkey breast-side down. After 30 minutes, turn the turkey over and arrange the bacon over the breast and legs. Roast for 3 hours, basting every 20 minutes with the giblet stock, then with the pan juices. Roast until the thickest part is 155°F on a meat thermometer. Let the turkey rest for 15 minutes before carving.

5. Make gravy by mixing 2 teaspoons cornstarch with ¼ cup water and blending with pan juices.

Roasting Turkeys

Always start the turkey breast-side down so the juices run into, rather than out of, the breast. The bacon prevents the breast from sticking to the roasting pan and adds a nice flavor to the juices. If, like most families, yours likes extra dressing (stuffing), make 3 to 4 cups extra and roast it in a casserole while you are roasting the turkey.

Stuffing for Roasted Turkey

Make your own GF cornbread for stuffing a day or two before, cube, and place in the refrigerator in a plastic bag until ready to use.

1. In a large frying pan, sauté the onion and celery in the butter. Add the sausage and break up with a wooden spoon. Cook until sausage is done and vegetables are tender. Place in a very large bowl.

2. Add the rest of the ingredients to the bowl. With gloves, or your hands inside large plastic bags, mix the ingredients well. Stuff your turkey with this mixture.

Makes stuffing for 1 turkey

1 onion, finely chopped
4 stalks celery with tops, finely chopped
4 tablespoons butter
1 pound bulk breakfast GF sausage
10 cups cubed GF cornbread
1 cup unsalted butter, melted with ½ cup water
2 teaspoons dried thyme
10 fresh sage leaves, minced, or 2 tablespoons dried
2 large tart apples, peeled, cored, and chopped
Salt and pure black pepper to taste

Stuffing for Roasted Chicken or Duck

Makes about 6 cups

1 cup chopped onion
2 cups chopped celery with
    tops
2 apples, peeled, cored, and
    chopped
4 tablespoons butter
1 cup pitted prunes, halved
¼ cup dry sherry mixed with
    ½ cup water
3 cups cubed GF cornbread
1 tablespoon dried rosemary
2 tablespoons minced orange
    or lemon zest
1 cup walnuts or pecans,
    toasted and chopped
Salt and pure black pepper
    to taste

Prunes and nuts go wonderfully well with duck and/or chicken. They give you the taste of fall in the country.

1. Sauté the onion, celery, and apples in the butter. When soft, place in a bowl. While the vegetables are sautéing, mix the prunes in a small bowl with the sherry and water to soak.

2. Toss all of the ingredients together. Use this to stuff the bird before roasting.

Tasty Turkey Parmesan

You can doctor your sauce with extra herbs, some lemon zest, and/or red wine.

1. Flatten the turkey pieces with a meat pounder. Cut into 4 serving pieces. Mix the cornbread crumbs with ½ cup Parmesan cheese. Dip the turkey in the flour, then in the egg, and finally in the crumb mixture.

2. Preheat oven to 350°F.

3. Fry turkey in oil until golden brown; drain on paper towels. Treat the baking dish with GF nonstick spray. Pour a little tomato sauce into the baking dish. Add the turkey pieces. Sprinkle with remaining ½ cup Parmesan cheese. Cover with tomato sauce. Spread the mozzarella over the top.

4. Bake in oven until hot and bubbling, about 20 minutes. Serve hot.

What's in the Stuffing?

The key to buying gluten-free food is reading every label carefully. Store-bought cornbread stuffing may have wheat flour mixed in with the corn flour and cornmeal. Corn muffins, also a favorite for making home-made stuffing, can have a mixture of wheat flour and cornmeal. In the long run, the safest way to provide gluten-free stuffing is to make the cornbread yourself.

Serves 4

1¼ pounds boneless, skinless turkey breast, sliced thin
1 cup GF cornbread crumbs
1 cup Parmesan cheese, divided
Salt and pure black pepper to taste
1 cup corn flour
1 beaten egg
1 cup oil for frying
2 cups GF tomato sauce
½ pound whole-milk mozzarella, shredded or thinly sliced

Mexican Chicken and Rice

Serves 4 to 6

½ cup corn flour
Salt and pure black pepper to taste
1 3½-pound chicken, cut in serving-sized pieces, rinsed and dried on paper towels
½ cup corn oil
4 cloves garlic, peeled and cut into thick slices
1 large red onion, chopped coarsely
4 tomatillos, peeled and chopped
1 hot pepper such as serrano or poblano, cored, seeded, and chopped
1 sweet red pepper, cored, seeded, and chopped
10 mushrooms, chopped
1½ cups chopped tomatoes (GF canned are fine)
1 cup dry red wine
1 lemon, thinly sliced, seeded
½ teaspoon cinnamon
1 cup short-grained rice
2 cups GF chicken broth
½ cup flat-leaf parsley or cilantro, chopped
3 cups cooked white rice

This dish is not too spicy, but it is well seasoned. Cook the rice while the chicken is simmering.

1. Mix the corn flour, salt, and pepper on a sheet of waxed paper. Dredge the chicken in it.

2. Heat the oil and brown the chicken in a large pan or Dutch oven. Remove the chicken from the pan.

3. Add the garlic, onion, tomatillos, hot pepper, sweet pepper, and mushrooms. Sauté until soft, about 10 minutes.

4. Add the mushrooms, tomatoes, wine, lemon, and cinnamon. Mix well.

5. Return the chicken to the pan, add short-grained rice and broth. Cover and simmer for 45 minutes. Just before serving, add the parsley or cilantro. Serve with rice.

Texas Influence

Mexican cooking is well seasoned, with layers of flavors coming from herbs, aromatic vegetables, and, yes, some spices. It's the Texas influence and the American passion for burning up the taste buds that has given Mexican cooking a reputation for being overly spiced.

Spicy Olive Chicken

You can make this in the pan with your baked or roasted chicken. The pan juices will add flavor to the sauce.

1. Sprinkle the chicken pieces with salt and pepper and brown them in the butter. Sauté the onion in the same pan. Add the broth, wine, and olives.

2. Using a fork, whisk in the mustard. Cover the pan and simmer until the chicken is done, about 45 minutes. Add salt, pepper, and hot sauce.

3. Pour sauce and olives over mashed potatoes, rice, or rice noodles. Garnish with chopped parsley.

Capers

Capers are flavorful berries. Picked green, they can be packed in salt or brine. Try to find the smallest—they seem to have more flavor than the big ones do. Capers are great on their own or incorporated into sauces. They are also good in salads and as a garnish on many dishes that would otherwise be dull.

Serves 4

1 3-pound chicken, cut into 8 pieces
Salt and pure black pepper to taste
4 tablespoons unsalted butter
⅔ cup chopped sweet onion
½ cup GF chicken broth
½ cup dry white wine
24 green olives, pitted
1 teaspoon prepared GF Dijon mustard
Salt, pure black pepper, and GF hot sauce to taste
Fresh parsley, chopped, for garnish

Vegetarian Entrées

chapter eight

Stuffed Artichokes with Lemon and Olives

Serves 4 as an entree or 8 as an appetizer

4 large artichokes, trimmed and split lengthwise
4 quarts water
½ lemon
1 cup cooked rice
10 green olives, chopped
10 kalamata olives, chopped
2 tablespoons minced parsley
3 tablespoons butter or margarine, melted
1 teaspoon garlic salt
Pure black pepper to taste
1 egg, optional

Artichokes have a way of making everything around them taste delicious. They can be eaten with just a little butter or GF mayonnaise or lemon juice.

1. Boil the artichokes in 4 quarts of water with lemon and rind, squeezed, for 20 minutes. Drain and lay on a baking sheet, cut-side up.

2. Preheat the oven to 350°F. Mix the rest of the ingredients (including the egg, if using) together in a large bowl.

3. Spoon the filling over the artichokes, pressing between the leaves. Bake for 15 minutes, until hot.

Grilled Portobello Mushrooms

These big, meaty mushrooms are great sliced over salad, stuffed, or chopped into sauce.

1. Marinate the mushrooms in the vinaigrette for 1 to 2 hours, covered, in the refrigerator.

2. Preheat your grill to glowing coals, or set your gas grill to low.

3. Grill mushrooms, then slice and serve.

Mushrooms and Protein

Mushrooms are not really high in protein, but they are filling. The large portobello mushrooms are great for grilling or stuffing with all kinds of goodies. They make excellent bases for rice, quinoa, eggs, and vegetables.

Serves 4

4 large (4 to 5 inches in diameter) portobello mushrooms, stems removed, brushed off
1 cup balsamic vinaigrette
Salt and pure black pepper to taste

Stuffed Peppers with Veggie-Burger Filling and Spices

Serves 4

4 large garlic cloves, minced
1 large onion, minced
¼ cup olive oil
1 tablespoon Asian sesame oil
1 pound GF veggie burgers
Salt and pure black pepper
  to taste
4 large green or red bell
  peppers

Veggie burgers are a boon to the vegetarian cook. They generally are well seasoned and quite delicious, but make sure to check the ingredients for a brand that is gluten-free.

1. Sauté the garlic and onion in the olive and sesame oil until soft. Add the veggie burgers, breaking up with a wooden spoon. Add salt and pepper.

2. Preheat oven to 350°F.

3. Cut the peppers in half lengthwise and scoop out seeds and cores. Fill with the burger mixture. Place on a baking sheet that you have prepared with GF nonstick spray.

4. Bake for 25 minutes. Serve hot.

Dry Veggie Burgers?

You can do several things to keep veggie burgers moist. Mixing a bit of chopped fresh tomato into the mix is one option. Another is to add olive oil, milk, or cream before grilling. A bit of cooked, mashed potatoes also adds bulk and moisture. Add about a tablespoon of tomato, oil, milk, or mashed potato per burger.

Stuffed Eggplant with Ricotta and Spices

This dish is also known as Eggplant Sicilian. It freezes beautifully and is very delicious.

1. Stack the salted eggplant slices on a plate and put another plate with a weight on top to press the brown liquid out of them.

2. Mix the flour and pepper and use it for dredging the eggplant slices. Fry the slices in the olive oil, removing to paper towels as they are browned.

3. Preheat oven to 325°F. Prepare a 2-quart casserole dish or a 10" x 10" glass pan with GF nonstick spray and spread with a thin layer of tomato sauce.

4. In a large bowl, mix the ricotta cheese, ½ cup of the Parmesan, eggs, and oregano. Place a tablespoon of the egg-cheese mixture on each slice of eggplant and roll, placing seam-side down in the baking dish.

5. Spread with sauce, sprinkle with the rest of the Parmesan and the mozzarella, and bake for 35 minutes.

Smaller Is Sweeter

The smaller eggplants now available are much sweeter and not old enough to have grown bitter. Also, many have few seeds. They come in pale cream, lavender, and purple, all the way from egg-sized to long and skinny. All are good!

Serves 4

- 2 medium eggplants, peeled, cut in 16 round slices (8 each) and salted
- 1 cup rice or corn flour
- Freshly ground black pepper to taste
- ¼ cup olive oil, or as needed
- 2 cups GF tomato sauce
- 1 pound ricotta cheese
- 1 cup grated Parmesan cheese, divided
- 2 eggs
- 1 tablespoon dried oregano
- 1 cup shredded mozzarella cheese

Stuffed Portobello Mushrooms with Roasted Tomatoes and Quinoa

Serves 4

4 portobello mushrooms, about 4 to 5 inches in diameter, stemmed and brushed off
16 cherry tomatoes, cut in half
¼ cup olive oil
1 tablespoon minced garlic
2 cups cooked quinoa
¼ cup walnuts, finely chopped (almonds or pecans are fine)
4 tablespoons butter or margarine, melted
1 teaspoon turmeric
Salt and pure red pepper flakes to taste
¼ cup capers (optional)
¼ cup golden raisins (optional)
1 teaspoon lemon zest (optional)

You can substitute rice for quinoa. However, you get a nice nutty flavor from the quinoa.

1. Preheat the oven to 350°F. Place the mushrooms on a well-greased baking pan.

2. Sprinkle the tomatoes with oil and garlic. Roast them in the oven for 20 minutes or until soft.

3. Mix the roasted tomatoes with the cooked quinoa, nuts, butter or margarine, and seasonings. Add optional ingredients if desired. Spoon into the mushrooms.

4. Bake the mushrooms for 30 minutes or until very hot and soft.

Do You Know Quinoa?

Rich, nutrient-filled quinoa is considered a "supergrain," though it is not really a grain but the starchy seed of a plant related to spinach. The protein in quinoa is more complete than that of grains and contains the amino acid lysine, as do buckwheat and amaranth. The quality of quinoa's protein is equivalent to that of milk.

Stuffed Portobello Mushrooms with Roquefort and Sweet Red Peppers

This is as good as it gets. Serve with salad or in an omelet.

1. Preheat your oven to 350°F. Place the marinated mushrooms on a baking sheet.

2. Place 2 tablespoons cheese in each mushroom. Put the pepper strips on top. Sprinkle with salt and pepper. Bake for 20 minutes, until the cheese melts.

Serves 4

4 large whole portobello mushrooms, marinated in balsamic vinaigrette
8 tablespoons crumbled Roquefort cheese
4 roasted red peppers, cut in strips (jarred is fine)
Salt and pure black pepper to taste

Indian Vegetable Cakes

Serves 4 to 6

1 tablespoon olive oil
1 (10-ounce) package frozen
    chopped spinach, thawed
    and squeezed of excess
    moisture
½ box (5 ounces) frozen baby
    peas, thawed
½ bunch scallions, chopped
1 teaspoon GF curry powder
Salt and GF hot pepper sauce
    to taste
¼ cup cornmeal
5 extra-large eggs, well
    beaten
½ cup Parmesan cheese

This is a great way to get kids to eat their veggies! A nonstick pan helps to prevent sticking. GF sour cream makes a very good garnish.

1. Heat olive oil in a nonstick pan over a medium flame. Mix together all ingredients except Parmesan cheese.

2. Drop patties, 3 or 4 at a time, into the pan and fry until delicately browned. Turn and sprinkle with cheese.

Sweet Potato Gratin with Leeks and Onions

The combination of sweet and savory makes this a fascinating, unique, and delicious dish.

1. Sauté the leeks, onions, and celery in olive oil or butter. Preheat the oven to 325°F. Prepare an oval metal or pottery gratin pan with GF nonstick spray.

2. Layer the sweet potato slices in the gratin pan with the vegetables. Sprinkle with thyme, salt, and pepper as you go along.

3. Finish with a layer of potatoes. Add the milk until it meets the top layer of potatoes. Then add the cornbread crumbs. Dot with extra butter or margarine.

4. Bake until the potatoes are soft, about 1 hour. Add more milk if it starts to dry out.

Serves 4 to 6

2 leeks, white part only, rinsed and chopped
2 large sweet onions such as Vidalias
2 stalks celery with tops, finely chopped
4 tablespoons olive oil or butter
1 teaspoon dried thyme
4 sweet potatoes, peeled and sliced thin
Salt and pure black pepper to taste
Milk to cover
1½ cups GF cornbread crumbs
Butter or margarine for topping

Corn and Spinach Pockets Stuffed with Cheese and Artichokes

Serves 8

1 10-ounce box frozen artichoke hearts
1 10-ounce box frozen spinach,
   thawed, moisture squeezed
   out
1 cup ricotta cheese
4 ounces cream cheese
¼ cup minced chives
¼ teaspoon freshly ground
   nutmeg
Salt and pure black pepper
   to taste
1 egg
8 large (8 to 9 inches in diameter) Corn Crepes (page 11)
Beaten egg for sealing
   pockets

This is one of the creative and exciting vegetarian and gluten-free dishes you can make
with Corn Crepes (page 11).

1. Cook the artichoke hearts until soft; whirl in
a food processor with spinach, slowly adding
the cheeses, chives, seasonings, and egg.

2. Preheat oven to 350°F. Lay out the crepes
on a nonstick baking sheet or one covered
with a sheet of aluminum foil.

3. Divide the filling among the crepes, spoon-
ing onto one half and leaving the other half
plain.

4. Wet the rims of the crepes with beaten egg.
Fold over and press lightly to seal, and then
bake for 20 minutes or until well browned and
filling is bubbling out.

Selecting and Preparing Artichokes

Look for artichokes that are tightly closed. Take
a pair of kitchen scissors and clip off the sharp
points. You can use a knife to cut off the tops.
They are hearty when stuffed with many kinds
of delicious foods. If you eat fish, salmon mixed
with rice makes an excellent stuffing.

Spinach with Baked Eggs and Cheese

This is an excellent brunch, lunch, or supper. Everyone loves it, and even after a tough day, it's easy to put together.

1. Preheat oven to 325°F. Prepare a 10" x 10" glass baking dish or gratin pan with GF non-stick spray. Sprinkle it with cornbread crumbs.

2. Mix the spinach, butter, cheese, nutmeg, and salt and pepper together. Stir in the heavy cream. Spread the spinach-cheese mixture in the bottom of the prepared pan.

3. Using the back of a tablespoon, make 8 depressions in the spinach mixture. Nest the raw eggs in their holes. Bake for 20 minutes or until the eggs are firm but not hard.

Serves 4

1½ cups GF cornbread crumbs
3 (10-ounce) packages frozen spinach, thawed, moisture squeezed out
2 tablespoons butter or margarine, melted
½ cup shredded Swiss cheese
½ teaspoon nutmeg
Salt and pure black pepper to taste
1 cup heavy cream
8 eggs

Crispy Potato Pancakes

Makes about 10 pancakes

4 Idaho potatoes, peeled and
  coarsely grated
2 mild onions, chopped fine
2 eggs, well beaten
½ cup potato flour
Salt and pure black pepper
  to taste
2 cups cooking oil (such as
  canola)
GF sour cream, applesauce,
  fruit preserves, GF salsa,
  or chutney to garnish

This is basically a good old kosher recipe. It is marvelous with applesauce, GF sour cream, or both. For brunch, it's excellent with eggs on the side.

1. Mix the grated potatoes, onions, and eggs in a bowl. Sprinkle with potato flour, salt, and pepper.

2. Heat the oil to 350°F and spoon in the potato cakes, pressing down to make a patty.

3. Fry until golden, about 5 minutes per side. Drain, keep warm, and serve with garnish of choice.

The Origins of Potato Pancakes

During the long winters in northern and eastern Europe, when fresh fruits and vegetables were not available, winter storage of carrots, potatoes, beets, Brussels sprouts, apples, and dried fruits was crucial to prevent scurvy, or ascorbic acid deficiency. As Mother Nature would have it, these vegetables are packed with vitamins and minerals. Potato pancakes with GF sour cream, applesauce, or fruit syrups became a staple in harsh climates.

Potato Frittata with Cheese and Herbs

Use both GF nonstick spray and butter in this recipe, or the starch in the potatoes will stick. You can experiment with different herbs and cheeses.

1. Using a mandoline, slice the potato as thin as possible. Prepare a heavy 12-inch pan, first with GF nonstick spray, then with butter.

2. Add the potatoes, making a thin layer, and season with salt and pepper. Cook over medium heat for 10 minutes—this will be the crust.

3. Beat the eggs well; add the cheese and minced sage. Pour over the potatoes and turn down heat to the lowest possible setting. Cook for 10 minutes.

4. When the eggs have set, run the frittata under the broiler until golden brown on top. Cut into wedges and serve at once with garnishes.

Striking Yukon Gold

Yukon Gold potatoes were developed in the 1970s at the University of Guelph, Ontario, Canada. They were initially slow to capture the market but now are widely popular, particularly suited for baking, salad, and soup.

Serves 4

1 large Yukon Gold potato, peeled
4 teaspoons butter
Salt and pure black pepper to taste
6 eggs
½ cup grated Parmesan cheese
6 sage leaves, minced
Fresh herbs, extra cheese, GF sour cream to garnish

Frittata with Asparagus and Two Cheeses

Serves 4

1 (10-ounce) box frozen chopped asparagus
2 tablespoons butter
6 eggs
1 cup grated Cheddar cheese
¼ cup shredded Monterey jack or pepper jack cheese
1 teaspoon lemon rind, minced
Salt and pure black pepper to taste

Some matches are made in heaven, and asparagus with eggs and cheese is a divine combination.

1. Cook the asparagus and drain it. If you are using fresh, trim off all of the woody ends and boil for 10 minutes; drain and chop.

2. Prepare a heavy 12-inch pan with GF nonstick spray and then melt the butter over medium-high heat. Beat the eggs; mix in the cheeses, lemon rind, and salt and pepper.

3. Pour the egg-cheese mixture into the pan, distribute asparagus, and reduce heat, cooking very slowly for 10 to 15 minutes.

4. Run under preheated broiler for 10 seconds, or until nicely browned.

Use Up Your Leftovers

The frittata is a staple in Italy—putting a lot of eggs together with leftover or fresh vegetables is a fine way of using every precious bit of food. A frittata can be jazzed up with herbs, cheeses, and hot red pepper flakes. Or it can be child-mild for young kids. The only thing to remember about frittatas is that just about anything goes!

Fried Potato Balls

You can hide surprises inside these treats, like olives, halved cherry tomatoes, or cubes of cheese.

1. Beat the egg yolks, 1 cup of the Parmesan cheese, flour, and salt and pepper into the potatoes. Fold in the egg whites.

2. Form into balls about the size of large marbles. Roll in Parmesan cheese. If too soft, place on a cookie sheet in the freezer for a few minutes.

3. Bring oil to 375°F. Carefully add the balls and fry until well browned.

4. Be careful not to let the oil get too hot. Drain on paper towels, and serve hot.

Make 8 to 12 balls

3 eggs separated, whites whisked stiff
1¾ cup finely grated Parmesan cheese, divided
¼ cup potato flour, more if the mixture is loose or wet
Salt and pure black pepper
1½ cups boiled riced potatoes
2 cups oil for frying

Tofu and Vegetables with Macadamia Nuts and Asian Citrus Sauce

Serves 4

1 tablespoon sesame seed oil

3 tablespoons peanut or other vegetable oil

1 bunch scallions, chopped

1-inch piece ginger root, peeled and minced

⅔ pound sugar snap peas, ends trimmed

2 cups mung bean sprouts

2 cups shredded Chinese cabbage

½ orange, juice and rind, pulsed in the food processor

1 teaspoon Chinese five-spice powder (check that it is GF)

1 teaspoon GF Chinese mustard or GF Japanese wasabi, or to taste

¼ cup sake or dry white wine

¼ cup light GF soy sauce

1 pound satin tofu, cubed

This is an elegantly flavored dinner with contrasting textures. Serve over rice.

1. Heat the oils in a wok. Add the scallions and ginger. Lightly mix in the rest of the vegetables and toss in the oil for 3 to 4 minutes. Place the vegetables in a large, warm serving bowl.

2. Mix together the orange juice and rind, five-spice powder, mustard, sake, and soy sauce.

3. Stir into the wok until blended. Add the tofu cubes and vegetables and mix to coat. Serve hot.

A Source of Protein for Vegetarians

Tofu, long used in Asia because meat and milk were both scarce and expensive, has become an important part of the vegetarian diet. It can be flavored to taste like many kinds of meat. Or it can be sweetened and prepared with fruit for desserts. It's delicious in soups and with vegetables.

Spinach-and-Cheese-Stuffed Baked Potatoes

This is an American favorite, and if you enjoy anchovies, they make a delightful addition to this recipe.

1. Preheat the oven to 350°F.

2. Bake the potatoes for 40 minutes. Then cool the potatoes and split them in half lengthwise.

3. Spoon out the insides of the potatoes and place in a bowl; add the spinach. Stir in the sour cream and nutmeg. Add the American cheese. Season to taste with salt and pepper.

4. Restuff the potato skins. Arrange the Cheddar cheese on top. Bake for another 20 minutes and serve hot.

**Serves 4 as a meal,
8 as a snack**

4 Idaho or Yukon Gold
   potatoes
1 (10-ounce) package frozen
   chopped spinach, thawed,
   moisture squeezed out
1 cup GF sour cream
¼ teaspoon nutmeg
1 cup grated white American
   cheese
Salt and pure black pepper
   to taste
½ cup shredded sharp Cheddar cheese

Sweet Pepper and Gorgonzola Omelet

Serves 2

2 teaspoons unsalted butter
4 eggs, well beaten
2 ounces crumbled Gorgon-
zola cheese
4" x 2" strips roasted red
pepper
Salt and pure hot red pepper
flakes to taste

This omelet has a delightful flavor from the Gorgonzola cheese melting into the eggs. A nonstick pan takes all of the guesswork out of making omelets.

1. Heat a 10-inch nonstick pan over medium-high heat. Melt the butter and swirl to coat. Add the eggs and swirl to distribute evenly in pan.

2. Place the cheese and pepper strips on one side of the omelet. Season with salt and pepper flakes.

3. Cook until just set, when it has the consistency of custard (soft and creamy but not liquid or runny). Flip the plain side over the side with the cheese and peppers. Cut in half and serve on a warmed plate.

Eggs

Eggs are a versatile, all-purpose protein. Omelets can solve any number of nutritional problems, plus providing something really easy to digest and great for finicky appetites. Various vegetables, cheeses, and herbs make perfect fillings for omelets. The more creative the combination, the more interesting the omelet.

Casseroles and Entrées

chapter nine

Beef Stroganoff

Serves 6

2 tablespoons olive oil

4 shallots, peeled and chopped

8 ounces tiny button mushrooms, brushed clean, stems removed

2 garlic cloves, minced

2 tablespoons tapioca flour plus ¼ cup for coating the meat

1 teaspoon dried mustard

Salt and pepper to taste

1½ cups beef broth, warmed

1 cup dry red wine

1 teaspoon GF Worcestershire sauce

2 pounds filets mignons, cut into bite-sized cubes

2 tablespoons unsalted butter

2 tablespoons snipped fresh dill weed

1 cup GF sour cream or crème fraîche

This is an elegant, historic recipe, named after the Russian general who is said to have invented it. You can serve it with potato pancakes on the side, or with wild rice.

1. In a large sauté pan, heat the oil over medium heat and add the shallots, mushrooms, and garlic. Cook for 5 minutes to soften. Add the flour, mustard, and salt and pepper, stirring to blend.

2. Mix in the warmed beef broth, cook, and stir to thicken. Stir in the wine and Worcestershire sauce and bring to a boil. Turn off the heat.

3. On a large piece of waxed paper, roll the beef in flour. Heat the unsalted butter in a separate pan. Sear the beef in the butter. Spoon the beef into the mushroom sauce, add the dill weed, and stir to blend. Simmer for 10 to 15 minutes; the beef should be medium-rare.

4. Just before serving, add the sour cream. Spoon over a bed of wild rice or serve with potato pancakes on the side.

Why Not to Wash Mushrooms

Mushrooms are grown in a safe and sanitary medium, often horse manure that has been treated with thermophilic bacteria. This kills any germs by naturally heating the growing medium to a very high temperature. Also, washing mushrooms makes them mushy because they absorb the water. Please don't peel them, either—just brush them off.

Las Chalupas with Crepe-atillas

You can make these delightful crepes in advance, then either refrigerate or freeze them. Fix them for a casual party for your family or for your teenager and friends.

1. Whirl the eggs, milk or water, salt, pepper, and flour in the blender. Whirl until smooth, stopping once to scrape down the sides of the jar. Let batter rest for 30 minutes or more. The flour may soak up extra liquid. The batter should be very loose, so if it's thick add extra milk.

2. Using a nonstick pan, heat the oil or melt the butter and fry eight 6-inch crepes until lightly golden on both sides. Set aside on waxed paper that you have sprinkled with flour.

3. Sauté the beef and onion, gradually adding the rest of the ingredients, except the toppings, and stirring until well blended.

4. Place the crepes on plates and let your guests add their favorite toppings.

Serves 4

2 eggs
1½ cups milk or water
½ teaspoon salt or seasoned salt (or to taste)
¼ teaspoon pepper (or to taste)
1 cup corn flour (masa harina)
Butter or cooking oil for frying tortillas/crepes
1 pound ground beef
1 small onion, chopped
2 pickled jalapeños, chopped, and 2 ounces of their juice
1 teaspoon salt and pepper to taste
1 teaspoon garlic powder
1 cup salsa
1 tablespoon chili powder
Salt and black pepper to taste
Toppings: 2 cups shredded jack cheese, 2 cups shredded Cheddar cheese, shredded iceberg or romaine lettuce, chopped tomato, chopped black or green olives, Guacamole (see page 271), 1 cup GF sour cream

Chestnut Cannelloni with Sage, Mushrooms, and Wine Sauce

Serves 6

2 eggs
1 teaspoon salt
Freshly ground white pepper to taste
1 cup milk
1 cup Italian chestnut flour
Vegetable oil or unsalted butter for cooking
1 cup ricotta cheese
2 eggs
¼ teaspoon nutmeg
½ cup smoked ham, thinly sliced and shredded
½ cup chopped fresh Italian flat-leaf parsley
½ cup freshly grated Parmesan cheese
2 shallots, minced
2 cups mushrooms, sliced
½ cup olive oil
1 tablespoon cornstarch
1 cup dry white wine
½ cup GF chicken broth
10 fresh sage leaves, chopped
Salt and pepper to taste
Grated Parmesan for the topping

The number of cannelloni you make depends not on the recipe but on how large and thick you make them. Plan on two stuffed tubes per person.

1. Put the eggs, salt, pepper, milk, and flour into the blender or food processor and whirl until smooth.

2. Heat plenty of oil or butter in a nonstick pan over medium heat. Pour the batter into the hot pan, moving the pan around in circles to evenly spread the batter.

3. Fry for a few minutes per side; don't over- or undercook or the pasta will tear. Stack on sheets of waxed paper and store in a plastic bag in the refrigerator until ready to use (if making it in advance).

4. Preheat oven to 350°F degrees.

5. Mix the ricotta, eggs, nutmeg, ham, parsley, and Parmesan in a bowl and, laying out the cannelloni, spread a tablespoon across one edge. Carefully roll the pasta into a tube and place in a buttered baking dish.

6. Sauté the shallots and mushrooms in the olive oil. Add the starch and stir until thickened. Blend in the wine and broth, sage, and salt and pepper. Pour over the cannelloni and sprinkle with cheese. Bake for 30 minutes.

Variation on a Theme

This is wonderfully delicious and easy to make in advance, and store for future use. A fine variation is to add some spinach to the ricotta stuffing. You can also substitute prosciutto ham for regular ham.

Savory Rice and Sausage

This is so easy and great for any time you are really busy. Kids love it and grown-ups do too.

1. Brown the sausage pieces, onion, and garlic. If the sausage is very lean, add a bit of olive oil to prevent the food from sticking.

2. Stir in the rice and toss with the sausage and vegetables. Add the broth and rosemary and cover. In a broiler-safe skillet or casserole dish, cook on very low heat or place in a 325°F oven for 45 minutes to 1 hour, depending on the type of rice you are using. (Do not use Minute rice.)

3. Just before serving, sprinkle the top with Parmesan cheese and brown under the broiler. Add the chopped parsley and serve.

The Old-Fashioned Ways

Once seasoned, a heavy black wrought-iron frying pan will last for generations. In fact, they never wear out. Since they're made of thick metal, they distribute heat evenly. Seasoning the pan requires just a skim of oil left on a warm pan overnight. Then, don't overuse detergent. Pass your pans on to your grandchildren, especially if yours came from your grandmother.

Serves 4 to 6

1 pound Italian sausage, sweet or hot, cut into 1-inch pieces
1 medium onion, chopped fine
2 cloves garlic, chopped
1 cup rice
2¾ cups GF chicken broth
1 teaspoon dried rosemary, or 1 tablespoon fresh rosemary
Parmesan cheese and chopped fresh parsley to garnish

Scalloped Potatoes with Leeks and Country Ham

Serves 6

1½ cups grated Parmesan cheese
1 cup coarsely grated Fontina cheese
½ cup corn flour
Salt and freshly ground black pepper to taste
6 Idaho or Yukon Gold potatoes, peeled and sliced thin
4 leeks, thinly sliced crosswise, white parts only
1 pound deli ham, sliced and then cut crosswise into dice
3 cups milk
4 tablespoons butter (for greasing baking dish and dotting on potatoes)

This is a great brunch or supper dish. It's filling and delicious, especially good on a cold day or nippy evening.

1. Grease a baking dish or prepare it with non-stick spray. Preheat oven to 350°F.

2. Mix together the cheeses, corn flour, salt, and pepper.

3. Place a layer of potatoes in the baking dish, then one of leeks, and dab with bits of ham. Sprinkle with the mixture of cheeses, corn flour, and spices. Repeat until you get to the top of the baking dish. Add the milk, sprinkle with cheese mixture, and dot with butter.

4. Bake for about 90 minutes. The top should be brown and crispy, the inside soft and creamy.

Tuscan Bean, Tomato, and Parmesan Casserole

When you are trying to whip up something satisfying, warming, and delicious for a cold and stormy night, this is it!

1. Fry the bacon until almost crisp. Place on paper towels to drain. Remove all but 1 teaspoon of bacon fat from frying pan. Add the oil, garlic, onion, and fennel. Sauté over low heat for 10 minutes, or until softened but not browned.

2. Preheat oven to 350°F. Blend the flour into the mixture and cook for 3 minutes, blending well.

3. Add the beans, tomatoes, and zucchini. Mix well and pour into a casserole dish. Add the herbs, red pepper flakes, and salt. Stirring, mix in the reserved chopped bacon.

4. Sprinkle Parmesan cheese and butter over the top and bake for 25 minutes, or until the cheese is lightly browned.

Eat More Beans

There are more varieties of legumes than it's possible to list here. They are delicious and loaded with protein, vitamins, minerals, and fiber. If a culture, or a household, needs to stretch its food supply, beans are the answer. They come in red and pink, green and orange, black and white, speckled or solid. Some have black eyes and others look like cranberries. Beans—legumes—are available in many sizes and shapes, from tiny peas to big kidneys.

Serves 4 to 6

4 slices GF bacon
¼ cup olive oil
4 cloves garlic, coarsely chopped
1 medium onion, peeled and coarsely chopped
½ fresh fennel bulb, coarsely chopped
1 tablespoon rice flour
2 cans white beans, drained and rinsed
16 ounces tomatoes, chopped (canned are fine)
1 medium zucchini, chopped
1 tablespoon chopped fresh basil
1 teaspoon dried oregano
½ cup fresh Italian parsley, rinsed and chopped
1 teaspoon dried red pepper flakes, or to taste
1 teaspoon salt, or to taste
½ cup freshly grated Parmesan cheese
2 tablespoons unsalted butter, cut into small pieces

Spaghetti Squash with Creamy Vodka and Shrimp Sauce

Serves 6

1 large (4 to 5 pounds) spaghetti squash, cooked
2 minced shallots
2 tablespoons olive oil
1 tablespoon butter
1 tablespoon cornstarch
½ cup vodka
1 28-ounce can GF crushed tomatoes
1 cup heavy cream
1½ pounds shrimp, peeled and deveined
Salt and plenty of freshly ground pepper to taste
½ cup each chopped fresh parsley and basil
¼ cup GF prosciutto ham, minced, for garnish

The squash can be prepared a day in advance. Its fresh taste lends itself to many sauces, from a tomatoey marinara to a meaty Bolognese.

1. Place the cooked squash in a large bowl and keep warm while you make the sauce.

2. Sauté the minced shallots in a mixture of oil and butter. When soft, add the starch. Cook and stir over low heat until well blended, then add the vodka and tomatoes.

3. Cover and simmer gently for 20 minutes.

4. Stir in the cream and heat slowly, then add the shrimp. Do not boil after the cream has been added. When the shrimp turns pink, pour over the spaghetti squash, and add salt and pepper to taste. Garnish with parsley, basil, and prosciutto.

Parmesan Cheese

Always grate Parmesan cheese yourself as you need it. Buy it in 1-pound blocks and keep well sealed with plastic wrap in the refrigerator. Try using a box grater for a coarse cheese with lots of body.

Hollandaise Sauce

If the sauce gets too hot, it will curdle. To fix, pour it back into the blender and add a tablespoon of boiling water, then whirl it for 30 seconds.

1. Melt the butter in a saucepan on the stove. While the butter is melting, place the lemon juice, egg yolks, egg, and cayenne in the jar of a blender.

2. When the butter has melted, reduce heat to very low. Very slowly pour the melted butter into the blender, set on low.

3. Return the sauce to the pan in which you heated the butter and stir constantly until thickened. Remove from heat; add salt and pepper. Serve immediately.

Makes 1½ cups

½ pound unsalted butter
Juice of 1 lemon
2 egg yolks plus 1 whole egg
⅛ teaspoon cayenne pepper
Salt and freshly ground black
    pepper to taste

Chicken Divan

1 pound broccoli florets, cut
  into bite-sized pieces,
  cooked, and drained
3 pounds chicken breasts,
  boneless and skinless, cut
  into strips
1 cup corn flour
1 tablespoon sea or kosher
  salt
Ground black pepper to taste
½ cup olive oil, or more as
  needed
1½ cups Hollandaise Sauce
  (see page 141)
2 tablespoons Parmesan
  cheese
Sprinkle of paprika (optional)

This is so exquisite that you won't miss potatoes, piecrust, or pasta. It stands alone as a
one-dish meal.

1. Make sure the cooked broccoli is well
drained. You can cook it in advance and place
it in the refrigerator on paper towels.

2. Roll the chicken in the flour, sprinkle with
salt and pepper. Preheat oven to 350°F.

3. Heat the olive oil in a sauté pan. Sauté the
chicken for 5 minutes on each side until golden
brown, adding more oil if the pan gets dry.

4. Either butter a 2-quart casserole or prepare
it with nonstick spray. Place the broccoli in the
bottom and spoon some Hollandaise over the
top. Arrange the chicken over the broccoli and
pour on the rest of the sauce. Sprinkle with
Parmesan cheese and paprika. Bake for 30
minutes.

Turkey and Fruit

Vary the flavors in this dish by adding fresh sage or fresh parsley. You can also substitute a variety of mushrooms for the fruit.

1. Melt the butter and add the onion and celery. Sauté until soft, about 10 minutes, over low heat. Add the fruit and seasonings. Cook until just tender, about 5 more minutes.

2. Preheat oven to 350°F.

3. Prepare a baking dish with nonstick spray. Sprinkle the turkey with salt and pepper and place it in a baking dish. Spread it with the fruit mixture.

4. Add the cider and broth. Sprinkle the top with cornbread crumbs and moisten with juice. Bake for 45 minutes.

Try it with Rice

More varieties of rice are now on the market. It used to be just Uncle Ben's and Carolina. Today, you can buy Arborio rice from Italy and basmati rice, the staple of the Indian and Chinese diets. You can also buy purple rice, brown rice, and sticky rice. Arborio and basmati rices are short grained and stubby. They make a lot more "cream" than other varieties do. Try them all and you will find favorites. Basmati and Arborio varieties are wonderful in risotto, baked rice, and rice pudding.

Serves 4

2 tablespoons butter
½ cup chopped sweet onion
2 stalks celery, rinsed and chopped
2 tart apples, peeled, cored, and chopped
2 ripe pears, peeled, cored, and chopped
½ cup dried cranberries
1 teaspoon dried thyme leaves
2 teaspoons dried rosemary spikes, crumbled
1¼ pounds sliced fresh turkey breast or thigh
Salt and pepper to taste
½ cup apple cider
½ cup GF chicken broth
1½ cups GF cornbread crumbs

Moroccan Eggplant and Lamb Casserole

Serves 4

2 large eggplants, peeled and
cut vertically into long, thin
slices
Table salt
1 red onion, peeled and diced
4 cloves garlic, peeled and
minced
¼ cup olive oil, more for
sautéing
1¼ pounds very lean ground
lamb
¼ teaspoon cinnamon
½ teaspoon ground coriander
seeds
Juice of 1 lemon
½ cup golden raisins (sultanas)
½ cup dried apricots, chopped
1 cup GF crushed tomatoes,
with their juice
10 fresh mint leaves, torn into
small pieces
Salt and pepper to taste
Hot paprika or cayenne to
taste

With this recipe, you don't have to worry
about a top crust or thickening. If you like it
thick, just add a bit of cornstarch or rice flour.

1. Slice the eggplant and stack it with plenty
of salt between the layers. Let it rest while you
prepare the filling.

2. Sauté the onion and garlic in a tablespoon
of olive oil. Add the lamb when the vegetables
are soft.

3. Add the rest of the ingredients and cook,
stirring until well blended. The apricots will
absorb much of the liquid. If still very loose,
sprinkle with a teaspoon of cornstarch. Cover
and simmer for 15 minutes.

4. Preheat oven to 350°F.

5. Drain any liquid from the eggplant and place
one layer in a well-oiled 11" x 13" baking dish.
Add some of the lamb mixture, distributing
carefully. Keep making layers until you have
one final layer of eggplant. Sprinkle with extra
oil and bake for 45 minutes. Serve in wedges.
The traditional accompaniment is rice.

Eggplants in Lavender, Purple, and White

Eggplants come in a number of sizes, shapes,
and colors—they taste pretty much the same.
The larger ones may have bitter seeds, and an
old method of sweetening them up is to peel
and cut them paper-thin, salt the slices on
each side, and stack them on a plate, under a
weight. Then, a lot of brown juice comes out,
and the slices are sweet.

Veal Loaf with Red Peppers and Gorgonzola

The water bath (or bain-marie) technique used here will make this tender meat loaf almost custard-like.

1. Preheat the oven to 325°F. Whirl the veal, onion, garlic, eggs, bread crumbs, oregano, salt, pepper, and chili sauce in a food processor until smooth.

2. Prepare a standard 9" x 5" bread pan with nonstick spray. Pour half of the mixture into the bread pan. Spread a layer of roasted red peppers on top and crumbled cheese over that. Add the rest of the veal mixture. Sprinkle with Parmesan cheese.

3. Place the bread pan inside of a large roasting pan, and add enough boiling water to come halfway up the sides of the bread pan. Place pans in oven and bake for 1 hour.

Basil

Basil is a versatile herb—raw or cooked, dry or fresh, it adds immeasurably to many main dishes, sauces, salads, and soups. In the old Italian lore, it was considered bad luck to chop basil with a knife—one was told to tear it carefully. The edges from tearing are not so clean and sharp, so perhaps they let more aroma and flavor out of the leaves. Basil also comes in a number of different varieties with different flavors. The standard Italian basil is fine for everything. At the end of the summer, pick all the basil, tie it in bunches, and let them dry. They will last all winter.

Serves 4 to 6

1½ pounds ground veal
1 small onion
2 cloves garlic
2 eggs
1 cup GF bread crumbs
1 tablespoon oregano
Salt and pepper to taste
½ cup GF chili sauce
2 roasted red peppers, packed in olive oil
3 ounces Gorgonzola cheese, crumbled
2 tablespoons grated Parmesan cheese

Zucchini with Seafood, Tomato, and Bacon

Serves 6

6 medium zucchinis
1 small onion, peeled and
    minced
2 cloves garlic, peeled and
    minced
1 serrano pepper, cored,
    seeded, and minced
2 tablespoons butter or olive
    oil
1 cup cooked rice
1 cup GF crushed tomatoes
1 pound crabmeat or imitation
    GF crabmeat
2 tablespoons freshly
    squeezed lemon juice
2 eggs
1 tablespoon dried oregano
    leaves or 2 tablespoons
    fresh oregano
Salt and pepper to taste
6 strips of GF bacon for
    garnish

This recipe can use up the baseball-bat-sized zucchinis, but it's better with the medium ones, about 10 to 12 inches each.

1. Cut the top quarter off of the zucchinis, lengthwise. Hollow out the zucchinis with the small side of a melon baller or with a half-teaspoon measuring spoon; reserve pulp.

2. Sauté the onion, garlic, pepper, and zucchini pulp in the butter until soft. Add all ingredients but the bacon.

3. Preheat the oven to 350°F.

4. Divide the filling among the zucchini boats. Lay a bacon strip on top of each stuffed zucchini. Place in a baking dish that you have prepared with nonstick spray or oil. Bake until the "boats" are hot and the bacon is brown and crisp. Serve hot or at room temperature.

Stuffed Vegetables

There are many vegetables you can successfully stuff with lots of different delicious ingredients. Chopped meat, shrimp, fish, and crabmeat make wonderful stuffings. A baked clam-stuffed mushroom is also a real treat. Ricotta cheese, used to stuff pastas such as ravioli and lasagna, also makes an excellent stuffing.

Vegetable Lasagna Primavera with Pasta Substitute

This recipe takes very little time and is excellent for a big family dinner. It's also great for vegetarians.

1. Mix the eggs, salt, pepper, milk, and corn flour in the blender and whirl until smooth.

2. Using a well-greased griddle, pour the batter, fry until firm, and cut into 10-inch strips that are 2 inches wide. Turn using an extra-large, long spatula. As you finish, place the strips on a baking dish that has been prepared with nonstick spray. When the bottom of the dish is covered, fry the rest of the batter in the same way and save it for topping.

3. In a bowl, mix the ricotta, extra eggs, Parmesan, vegetables, and parsley. Spread in tablespoonfuls over the base in the dish. Cover with more of the pasta strips.

4. Add the cream sauce and cover with shredded mozzarella. Bake for about 12 minutes. Serve hot.

A Versatile Pasta

Any sauce that you would use on wheat pasta can be used on corn pasta—from a rich Alfredo sauce to a robust marinara sauce.

Serves 6 to 8

2 eggs
½ teaspoon table salt or sea salt (or to taste)
¼ teaspoon pepper (or to taste)
1½ cup milk or water
1 cup corn flour (masa harina)
Butter or oil for greasing the griddle
2 cups chopped raw mixed fresh vegetables such as scallions, zucchini, fresh spinach, and young peas
½ cup finely chopped fresh parsley
1½ cups Basic Cream Sauce (see page 176)
1 lb. ricotta cheese
½ cup Parmesan cheese
2 eggs
1 cup shredded mozzarella cheese

Chicken in Apple Cider and Brandy

Serves 4 to 6

2 small chickens, cut into quarters
4 tablespoons butter
1 cup chopped onion
1 tablespoon cornstarch
¼ cup apple brandy or apple jack
1¼ cups apple cider
Salt and pepper to taste
½ cup heavy cream

You can prepare this dish in advance. Reheat when you're ready to serve, adding the cream at the last minute.

1. Rinse and pat the chicken dry. Brown it in butter over medium heat. Add the onion and cook until softened. Stir in the cornstarch.

2. Add the brandy and flame it by setting it on fire with a long match. Be careful not to burn yourself. Add the cider and salt and pepper. Cover and simmer for 25 minutes.

3. Just before serving, place the chicken on a platter. Add the cream to the sauce in the pan, and heat. Spoon sauce over chicken, sprinkle with your favorite herbs, and serve.

Shirred Eggs and Asparagus au Gratin

This is a very easy brunch or supper dish. You can use frozen asparagus, but fresh is better. The trick is arranging the asparagus evenly in the pan.

1. Blanch the asparagus in boiling water for 5 minutes. Shock in ice water and drain. Preheat oven to 350°F.

2. Prepare a gratin pan or dish with nonstick spray and arrange the asparagus in the bottom. Break the eggs over the top. Sprinkle with Roquefort and bake until eggs are done and cheese is hot and runny (about 12 minutes). Serve hot.

Serves 4

1 pound fresh asparagus, ends trimmed, or 2 (10-ounce) packages frozen
8 eggs
1 cup crumbled Roquefort cheese

Asian Dishes

chapter ten

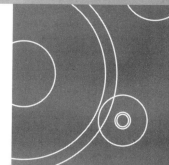

Asian-Style Soup with Rice Noodles

Serves 4

1 quart GF chicken broth
2 cloves garlic, minced
1 inch fresh ginger root,
   peeled and minced
1 bunch scallions, thinly sliced
12 canned water chestnuts
1 cup bean sprouts, well
   rinsed
½ cup dry sherry
½ cup GF soy sauce
½ pound satin tofu
2 cups rice noodles, cooked
12 snow peas, sliced on the
   diagonal, for garnish

This can be served in small bowls as a first course or in large bowls as lunch. The contrast between soft and crunchy, spicy and sweet, makes this interesting.

1. Bring the chicken broth to a boil and add all but the tofu, noodles, and snow peas. Cover and simmer for 10 minutes. Add the tofu.

2. Stir gently and add the cooked noodles. Garnish with the snow peas and serve.

Soy Galore

Tofu is made of soy and is related to all soy products, such as soy sauce, soy nuts, and soy paste. All are excellent food supplements. Tofu comes in satin (very soft and custardy), medium, and firm. The firm is excellent fried. The more tofu you eat, the better off your arteries will be—it has no cholesterol.

Shrimp and Coconut Soup

This is equally good served chilled or hot. You can add 1 cup of cooked rice to this, but it is not necessary.

1. Sauté the shallots in the oil until soft, about 10 minutes over medium heat. Stir in the cornstarch and cook until very thick.

2. Add the liquid ingredients and cook, covered, over very low heat for 30 minutes.

3. Stir in the rice and shrimp; heat until the shrimp turns pink. Add salt and white pepper to taste and serve hot or cold.

Shrimp Shell Broth

Shrimp Shell Broth makes a flavorful addition to seafood soup. Next time you are preparing shrimp, reserve the shells. Add 1 cup of water, 1 cup of wine, and a bay leaf to the shells from a pound of shrimp. Bring to a boil, lower heat, and simmer, covered, for 20 minutes. Strain and use as broth in your soup.

Serves 4

2 shallots, minced
2 teaspoons peanut oil or other vegetable oil
2 tablespoons cornstarch
1½ cups Shrimp Shell Broth (see this page), warmed
½ cup dry white wine
1 cup unsweetened coconut milk
1 cup cooked rice (optional)
1 pound shrimp, shelled and deveined, chopped
Salt and freshly ground white pepper to taste

Spinach Soup with Puffy Dumplings

Serves 4

1½ quarts GF chicken broth (canned is fine)
1 8-ounce package fresh baby spinach, shredded, or 1 10 ounce package frozen, thawed and squeezed to remove moisture
¼ cup fresh lemon juice
¼ cup dry white wine
¼ cup GF soy sauce
1 teaspoon sugar
1 teaspoon Thai green chili sauce, or to taste
¼ teaspoon ground coriander
Minced rind of ½ lemon for garnish
1 recipe Puffy Dumplings (see page 155)

You can add other shredded vegetables to this soup, such as watercress, Chinese cabbage (also called Napa cabbage), or snow peas.

1. Bring the chicken broth to a boil and add the shredded spinach. Simmer for 10 minutes and add the rest of the ingredients, except the dumplings.

2. Float the dumplings on top of soup. Cover and cook for 2 minutes, turning dumplings after 2 minutes.

Garnishes Transform Simple Soups

If your soup seems a bit blah, try adding seasoned salt or float fresh herbs like chives, oregano, or parsley on top. Tasty GF crackers can be added to the soup too, as well as various kinds of cheese.

Puffy Dumplings

These can be used in any soup you like—not only in Asian recipes, but also in Mediterranean vegetable soups and even in Hungarian goulash.

1. Mix the dry ingredients in a bowl; stir in the milk and egg until a stiff dough is formed.

2. Drop by half-teaspoonfuls into hot soup. Stir gently so that the dumplings cook evenly.

Serves 4

¼ cup rice flour
1 teaspoon GF baking powder
½ teaspoon black pepper, or to taste
1 teaspoon dried chopped chives
4–5 teaspoons milk
1 egg, beaten

Rice Flour Crepes

Serves 4

2 eggs
1½ cups water or milk
½ teaspoon salt
¼ teaspoon freshly ground
   white pepper
1 cup rice flour
Peanut or canola oil

Use milk instead of water if you want a richer crepe.

1. Place the eggs, water, and salt in a blender. Add pepper and flour, stopping once to scrape the sides of the jar.

2. Oil a nonstick pan, set heat to medium, and slowly pour or ladle small amounts of the batter into the pan, lifting and tipping to spread the batter.

3. When the edges start to get brown, flip the crepe. Cook for only a minute on the reverse side or it will become crisp and not pliable.

4. Cool and stack between sheets of waxed paper.

Crepes, Pancakes, Tortillas, and Cannelloni—Ripe for the Stuffing

While gluten-free flours can be a disaster under certain circumstances, they are a great success when it comes to crepes, pancakes, and corn tortillas, which are made like crepes. You can stuff them like wontons, make tubes and fill them, or fold them and dip them into a spicy sauce. Experiment.

Stir-Fried Shrimp and Vegetables in Rice Crepe Wraps

These are great stuffed or stacked with filling between the layers. Or try dipping them in teriyaki sauce.

1. Heat the sesame and peanut oil in a wok or frying pan and add the vegetables and shrimp. Stir and cook until the shrimp turn pink. Add the rest of the ingredients except for the crepes and the egg. Mix until well sauced.

2. Place the shrimp and vegetables in a bowl and cool. Put a spoonful of filling on half of a crepe. Paint the rim of the circle with the beaten egg. Fold over and press to seal.

3. Broil on high heat or steam the filled crepes for 10 minutes or until they are steaming hot. Serve hot.

Serves 4

1 tablespoon sesame oil
¼ cup peanut oil
4 scallions
4 garlic cloves
1 zucchini squash, finely chopped
1 onion, finely chopped
⅔ pound raw shrimp, shelled and deveined
½ cup almonds, chopped
1 tablespoon fish sauce
¼ cup dry sherry
1 teaspoon Wasabi powder mixed with 2 teaspoons water to make a paste
1 recipe for Rice Flour Crepes (see page 156)
1 egg, beaten

Spicy Beef-Stuffed Mushrooms

Serves 4

½ pound chopped sirloin
½ cup minced onion
2 cloves garlic, minced
1 inch ginger root, peeled and
minced
2 tablespoons cooking oil
1 tablespoon GF Worcestershire sauce
1 egg, slightly beaten
Salt and freshly ground black
pepper to taste
12–16 large mushroom caps,
stems removed, brushed off

The mushrooms should be 2½ inches across. This is a great side dish or appetizer. Served over salad greens, stuffed mushrooms make a fine lunch.

1. Sauté the meat, onion, garlic, and ginger in the oil, mixing constantly to break up lumps. When the meat turns pink (but not gray or brown), remove from the heat and add the Worcestershire sauce, taste, and add salt and pepper. When almost cool, blend in the egg.

2. Preheat the oven to 350°F. Divide the stuffing between the mushrooms in a baking pan. Pour enough water to come ¼ inch up the sides in the pan.

3. Bake the mushrooms for 25 minutes. You can sprinkle them with chopped fresh herbs of your choice when done.

Peanut Dipping Sauce for Satay

This is excellent with chicken, beef, pork, or lamb. It can be made in advance and reheated at the last minute.

1. In the food processor, whirl the coconut milk, peanuts, lemon or lime juice, brown sugar, soy sauce, and chili oil. Process until very smooth.

2. Heat the peanut oil in a large saucepan. Add the onion and garlic and cook over medium heat until just soft, about 3 minutes.

3. Pour the peanut mixture into the pan and mix well. Heat on low, but do not boil.

Wooden Skewers Must Be Soaked!

Wooden skewers must be soaked or they will burn when on the grill or under the broiler. Place them in a pan of water for an hour. You can also get very fancy skewers with decorative handles or metal at the ends. Simple metal skewers are also available. When using metal skewers, be sure to oil them or use nonstick spray to keep the food from sticking.

Makes about 2 cups (enough for 12 skewers of meat)

½ cup unsweetened coconut milk
1 cup dry-roasted peanuts
1 tablespoon lemon or lime juice
1 tablespoon dark brown sugar, or more to taste
1 tablespoon GF dark soy sauce
½ teaspoon chili oil, or to taste
2 tablespoons peanut oil
2 tablespoons finely chopped sweet onion
2 cloves garlic, minced

Serves 4

1½ pounds boneless, skinless chicken breast
½ cup GF soy sauce
2 teaspoons Thai red chili paste, or to taste
2 tablespoons minced fresh gingerroot
1 tablespoon sesame oil
2 tablespoons dry sherry

The chicken or other meat for satay should be grilled over hot coals. You can use tender beef instead of chicken. The marinade is good with any meat.

1. Set twelve 10-inch skewers to soak in water to cover for at least 40 minutes. Rinse the chicken, pat it dry, and cut it into bite-sized pieces.

2. Mix the rest of the ingredients together and add the chicken. Cover and marinate for 2 hours.

3. String the chicken on the skewers and grill over glowing coals for 4 to 5 minutes per side. Serve with any of the dipping sauces listed in this chapter.

Spicy Sesame Sauce for Lamb, Chicken, or Falafel

Tahini, sesame-seed paste, is the basis of this delicious sauce. Use it as a dipping sauce for any meat, fish, or shellfish.

Mash garlic and salt together to make a paste. Add the rest of the ingredients and blend well. Store, covered, in the refrigerator.

Makes 1½ cups

1–2 cloves garlic, minced
1 teaspoon salt, or to taste
½ cup tahini
¼ cup lemon juice
¼ cup water
¼ cup peanut or olive oil
2 tablespoons chopped fresh
   parsley or cilantro
¼ teaspoon ground cumin

Ginger and Spice Dipping Sauce

Makes 1½ cups

1 cup GF soy sauce
1 tablespoon minced fresh
ginger root
1 tablespoon fresh lime juice
1 tablespoon concentrated
pineapple juice
2 tablespoons GF English
mustard

This is an all-purpose dipping sauce or marinade.

Mix all ingredients together. Serve with just about anything.

Bits and Bites in Asian Cooking

One of the most delightful things about a great deal of Asian cooking is that you aren't stuck with an overloaded plate stacked with just one thing. In much the same way that Latin cooking employs wraps, many Asian cuisines use lettuce and other leaves for wrapping food. This is a great way to enhance a gluten-free diet.

Chinese-Style Crab in Red Chili Sauce

Ever since Marco Polo brought pasta to Italy, Italians and the rest of the world have loved it. This dish could have been one that old Polo loved.

1. Heat the oil in a large frying pan or wok.

2. Add the vegetables and stir-fry for 3 minutes. Then stir in the soy, tomatoes, crabmeat, and wine.

3. Boil noodles according to package directions, then add to the sauce and let the liquid soak in. Serve hot.

Serves 4

¼ cup peanut oil
4 cloves garlic, minced
1 bunch scallions, minced
2 inches of fresh gingerroot, peeled and minced
4–6 Scotch bonnet chilies, or to taste, cored, seeded, and minced
¼ cup GF dark soy sauce
2 fresh tomatoes, rinsed, cored, and chopped
1 cup canned crabmeat
½ cup dry white wine or rice wine
1 8-ounce package medium-thick rice noodles

Sesame-Crusted Chicken Breasts

Serves 4

¼ cup pineapple juice
¼ cup orange juice
1 tablespoon lime juice
½ cup GF soy sauce
1 inch ginger root, peeled and minced
2 cloves garlic, or to taste, minced
1 teaspoon chili oil, or to taste
2 large boneless, skinless chicken breasts, halved
1 egg, beaten
½ cup sesame seeds

Serve this with rice and lots of vegetables. Leftovers can be chopped, mixed with a spicy sauce, and used to fill Rice Flour Crepes (page 156) as a delicious snack.

1. In a nonreactive bowl or glass pan large enough to hold the chicken, whisk together the juices, soy sauce, ginger, garlic, and chili oil. Rinse the chicken breasts and pat dry with paper towels. Add the chicken to the sauce and turn to coat. Cover and refrigerate for 4 hours.

2. Drain the chicken; dip in beaten egg and then in sesame seeds. Grill or sauté in oil for 6 minutes per side, depending on thickness of meat. Serve hot.

Chili and Other Hot Sauces

Chinese, Indians, and other groups in Asia, Southeast Asia, and Asia Minor make their own versions of chili for cooking. Chili oil is extremely hot. Chili paste comes in green and red and is popular in Thailand. The Chinese make a chili-and-garlic paste called Sichuan chili. Tabasco sauce, fresh chopped chilies (red and/or green), cayenne pepper, and red pepper flakes can be substituted.

Roasted Cornish Game Hens with Ginger-Orange Glaze

This is a snap and tastes wonderful. It makes a delicious, but sticky, picnic.

1. Preheat oven to 375°F.

2. Rinse hens, pat dry with paper towels, brush with olive oil, and sprinkle with salt and pepper.

3. Stir the rest of the ingredients together in a small saucepan over low heat to make glaze; set aside.

4. Roast hens in a baking dish or pan, cut-side up, for 15 minutes. Turn hens and brush with glaze. Continue to roast for another 20 minutes, brushing hens with glaze every 5 minutes.

Fresh Gingerroot

You can use fresh gingerroot in all kinds of dishes, from dinners to desserts. Dried ground ginger, ginger snaps, and candied ginger are often used in cooking. Unpeeled fresh ginger freezes beautifully and can be added to sauces, salad dressings, and desserts such as puddings. When you want to use it, cut off an inch or two and peel it, then grate it, mince it, or finely chop it.

Serves 4

2 Cornish game hens, split
2 tablespoons olive oil
Generous sprinkle of salt and pepper
1 tablespoon orange marmalade
2 tablespoons peanut oil
1 tablespoon GF soy sauce
2 tablespoons orange juice
1 tablespoon minced fresh gingerroot

Curried Shrimp with Avocados

Serves 4

¾ cup GF mayonnaise
2 teaspoons GF curry powder
Juice of 1 lime
1 teaspoon GF hot chili oil or
    hot pepper sauce such as
    Tabasco
½ pound raw medium shrimp,
    peeled and deveined
4 ripe avocados, halved,
    peeled, and pitted
Hungarian sweet or hot
    paprika to taste
Dry-roasted peanuts, for
    garnish

Adapting Asian flavors to American lifestyles can produce delightful dishes such as this. Quick and simply made, it's a fine lunch or light supper served with rice.

1. Preheat oven to 350°F.

2. Mix the mayonnaise with the curry, lime juice, and hot chili oil. Chop the shrimp and mix it with the mayonnaise sauce.

3. Place the avocado halves in a baking dish coated with nonstick spray. Spoon the shrimp and sauce mixture into the avocados. Sprinkle with paprika and peanuts.

4. Bake the shrimp-stuffed avocados for 20 minutes. You can vary this by adding chopped tart apple, pineapple, or red grapes.

How Hot Is Too Hot?

Any supermarket has dozens of bottles of various kinds of hot sauce, from Jamaican to Chinese to African to, of course, Asian. The degrees of heat and other flavorings such as garlic, ginger, et cetera, vary. However, for the flavors of the food to come through, use only as much as you find adds piquancy—don't burn your tongue or you will kill valuable taste buds.

Curried Lamb Grilled on Skewers

Try grilling these and serving with the Spicy Sesame Sauce (page 161).

1. Mix the first six ingredients together in a bowl. Add the lamb and turn to coat with marinade. Cover and refrigerate for 2 hours.

2. Soak 8 to 10 wooden skewers for at least 40 minutes. String the lamb on the skewers and grill over hot coals for 4 minutes per side. Serve hot.

Serves 4

½ cup peanut oil
1 teaspoon GF curry powder
2 tablespoons lemon juice
4 cloves garlic, minced
½ teaspoon ground coriander
2 teaspoons hot sauce, or to taste
1 pound bite-sized lamb chunks, from the leg or shoulder

Lobster
with Sherry Sauce

Serves 4 to 6

4 chicken lobsters, 1–1¼
  pounds each
1 teaspoon Asian five-spice
  powder
1 clove garlic, minced
¼ cup sesame seed oil
¼ cup sherry
Juice of ½ lemon
2 tablespoons minced ginger
  root

This adaptation is a unique way to serve lobster. Garnish with fresh lemon wedges.

1. Boil the lobsters for 20 minutes, then split them and crack the claws.

2. Preheat the broiler to 500°F.

3. Mix the rest of the ingredients together in a saucepan to make the sauce. Bring to a boil and spoon over the lobsters.

4. Broil for 3 minutes. Serve.

Snow Peas with Water Chestnuts and Ginger

This tasty side dish is very fast and good. It's a boon to the busy working person who wants fresh vegetables but has little time.

1. Place the snow pea pods in a hot wok or frying pan with the oil. Stir to coat, then add the water chestnuts and peanuts, stirring again.

2. Continue cooking, and after 5 minutes, add the rest of the ingredients. Mix well and serve hot or at room temperature.

Cheese and Milk in Asian Cooking

The reason that cheese and milk are practically nonexistent in Asian cooking is that Asian countries do not have many dairy cows. In some areas, water buffalo work hard and produce milk too. Water buffalo in Italy provide the milk for a wonderful mozzarella cheese. Asians substitute tofu for meat, and what meat they do eat is stretched with vegetables and rice. Fish is popular in lake and seaside communities. Americans have adapted Asian flavors in a popular fusion food.

Serves 4

1 pound snow pea pods, ends trimmed
½ cup peanut oil
1 (8-ounce) can water chestnuts, drained, rinsed, and sliced
½ cup unsalted peanuts
2 tablespoons GF soy sauce
1 teaspoon lemon juice
1 tablespoon minced fresh gingerroot
Tabasco or other red pepper sauce

Rich and Thick Chicken Curry with Peppers

Serves 4

2 cloves garlic, minced
½ red onion, finely chopped
1 sweet red pepper, cored,
    seeded, and finely chopped
1 sweet green bell pepper,
    cored, seeded, and finely
    chopped
½ cup peanut or olive oil
1 pound skinless, boneless
    chicken breasts, cut into 8
    serving pieces
½ cup rice flour
1 tablespoon salt and ground
    black pepper to taste
24 tiny button mushrooms,
    cleaned, ends trimmed
2 tablespoons GF Madras
    curry powder
3 tablespoons cornstarch
1 cup GF chicken broth,
    warmed
1 cup heavy cream
½ cup chopped parsley or
    cilantro
3 cups cooked white or brown
    rice
Chopped fresh fruit, peanuts,
    and chutney to accompany

This is a British adaptation of an Indian curry. Serve over rice (white or brown) and with Major Grey's chutney, which is available almost everywhere.

1. Sauté the garlic, onion, and peppers in the peanut oil. Dredge the chicken in rice flour, salt, and pepper. Add to the vegetables and cook over medium heat for 2 minutes per side, until just golden.

2. Stir in the mushrooms. Mix in the curry powder and cornstarch. Add the warmed chicken broth and stir until smooth and very thick. Add the cream.

3. Cover and cook over very low heat, being careful not to boil. Garnish with parsley or cilantro and serve over rice with plenty of condiments on the side.

Cold Cellophane Noodle Salad with Crabmeat

Cellophane noodles do not usually need to be cooked separately in lots of water. They are very thin and made from mung bean flour.

Mix the vinegar, oil, and soy sauce in a large salad bowl. Add the garlic and lemon rind, crabmeat and noodles. Mix well, toss in the rest of the ingredients, and serve.

Asian Noodles— Most Are Gluten-Free!

Take your glasses to an Asian market and check the labels on the rice noodles. You'll find that almost all are made with rice, only rice, and not wheat flour. You can use these noodles in soups or in place of pasta. Also, we urge you to try spaghetti squash if you haven't already—it holds up well, is easy to prepare, and is delicious!

Serves 4

1 (6-ounce) package cellophane noodles, cooked according to package directions
2 tablespoons rice wine vinegar
½ cup peanut oil
¼ cup GF light soy sauce
2 cloves garlic, minced
Rind of 1 lemon, minced
1 cup julienned jicama
Juice of 1 lemon
2 cups shredded Chinese (Napa) cabbage
1 long cucumber, peeled and julienned
1 pound cooked crabmeat (Maryland blue crab is best)

Chinese Cabbage with Sesame

Serves 4

2 tablespoons sesame oil
2 tablespoons canola or other light oil
1 tablespoon sesame seeds
1 1½-pound head Chinese (Napa) cabbage, washed and thinly sliced
Juice of ½ lemon
2 cloves garlic, minced
Salt, pepper, and GF soy sauce to taste

Chinese cabbage, also called Napa cabbage, is wonderful cooked, or served raw in salads. It's pale green, mild, leafy, and very good for you!

1. Place the oils in a hot wok or frying pan. Add the sesame seeds and toast for 2 minutes.

2. Stir in the cabbage, lemon juice, and garlic. Toss until just wilted, about 4 minutes. Add the seasonings and serve.

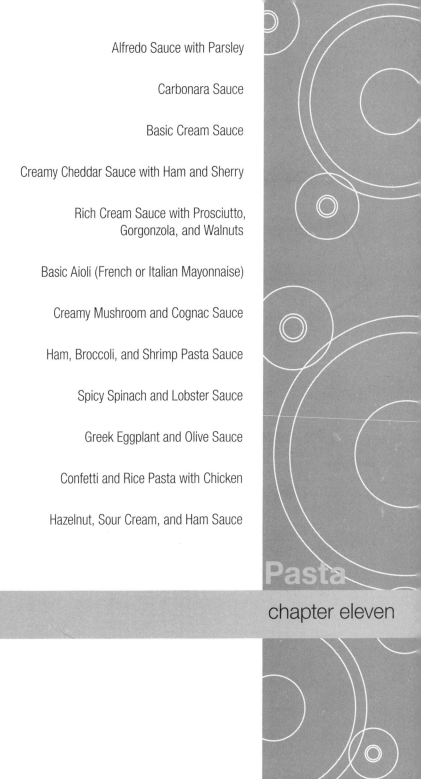

Alfredo Sauce with Parsley

Carbonara Sauce

Basic Cream Sauce

Creamy Cheddar Sauce with Ham and Sherry

Rich Cream Sauce with Prosciutto,
Gorgonzola, and Walnuts

Basic Aioli (French or Italian Mayonnaise)

Creamy Mushroom and Cognac Sauce

Ham, Broccoli, and Shrimp Pasta Sauce

Spicy Spinach and Lobster Sauce

Greek Eggplant and Olive Sauce

Confetti and Rice Pasta with Chicken

Hazelnut, Sour Cream, and Ham Sauce

Pasta

chapter eleven

Alfredo Sauce
with Parsley

Makes 1½ cups

1 tablespoon unsalted butter
2 tablespoons minced shallots
1 cup heavy cream
1 cup baby peas, frozen are
    fine (optional)
½ cup grated Parmesan
    cheese
2 large eggs
1 tablespoon cracked pep-
    percorns, or to taste
Salt to taste
½ cup chopped fresh parsley

The eggs in Alfredo sauce are generally cooked by the hot GF pasta sauce or mixed with the GF "pasta" to cook.

1. Melt the butter and sauté the shallots for 3 to 4 minutes. Add the heavy cream. (If using the baby peas, cook in the hot cream.) Bring to a boil and thicken, cooking for about 6 minutes, stirring constantly.

2. Remove from the heat and stir in the cheese. In a separate, large serving bowl, beat the eggs. Whisk in a tablespoon of the cream sauce; stirring constantly, add the remainder of the sauce, a little at a time. (Be careful—if you put the hot GF sauce into the eggs too quickly, they will scramble.)

3. Add pepper, salt, and parsley. Pour over spaghetti squash or rice noodles.

Cracked Peppercorns

When a recipe calls for cracked or coarsely ground black pepper, there's an easy way to prepare it. Place a tablespoon or so of pepper-corns on a chopping board. Press a heavy frying pan down on the peppercorns and rock it around gently. You will then have cracked pepper. Many pepper grinders also have a setting for coarse grind. You generally have to loosen the screw at the top of the grinder to make the pepper coarse.

Carbonara Sauce

This is not for someone on a diet; however, it's very delicious and easy to make.

1. Cook the bacon over low heat until it is fried crisp, then remove it to paper towels and crumble. Reserve the fat. Sauté the shallots in the bacon fat. Add the black pepper and cream. Bring to a boil and cook over medium-low heat until thick.

2. Mix the eggs and cheese in a bowl. Add a tablespoon of sauce, whisking. Continue to add sauce slowly, whisking constantly. Add the parsley, crumbled rosemary, reserved bacon, and pepper.

3. Pour over rice noodles or spaghetti squash. (You probably won't need salt because there's salt in the bacon.)

Carbonara Fan

The origins of carbonara are found in Italy, but whether it comes from Rome or the Lazio region is uncertain. Food writer Calvin Trillin, author of *The Tummy Trilogy*, is such a fan of carbonara sauce that he suggested it replace turkey as the American Thanksgiving Day holiday dish.

Makes 1½ cups

4 strips GF bacon
4 shallots, minced
2 teaspoons coarsely ground pure black pepper
1 cup heavy cream
2 eggs, beaten
½ cup grated Parmesan cheese
¼ cup chopped fresh parsley
1 tablespoon fresh rosemary, or 1 teaspoon dried, crumbled
1 teaspoon cracked black peppercorns, or to taste

Basic Cream Sauce

Makes 2 cups

3 tablespoons unsalted butter
3 tablespoons corn flour
2 cups milk or cream, warmed
Salt and pure black pepper
    to taste

Optional: ⅛ teaspoon nutmeg, 1 teaspoon GF Dijon mustard, or 1 tablespoon snipped fresh chives. This cream sauce is the basis for a lot of cooking. You can use milk instead of cream, but don't substitute margarine for butter.

1. Melt the butter and stir in the flour. Sauté, stirring for 4 to 5 minutes over medium-low heat. Add the warm milk or cream, whisking constantly until thickened to desired consistency.

2. Just before serving, add salt and pepper. Optional ingredients can be added at this time.

Beyond the Basics

Once you learn to make a basic cream sauce, you can add GF mustard, sautéed mushrooms, oysters, shrimp, herbs, and all kinds of luscious things. You can pour the sauce over fish or shellfish, poultry, and/or vegetables.

Creamy Cheddar Sauce with Ham and Sherry

This is excellent over vegetables, spaghetti squash, or rice.

1. Melt the butter and stir in the flour. Sauté, stirring for 4 to 5 minutes over medium-low heat. Add the warm milk or cream, whisking constantly until thickened to desired consistency.

2. Remove from the heat and stir in the cheese, ham, sherry, and salt and pepper. Serve.

Sherry as a Flavoring

There are several kinds of sherry used in cooking, ranging from very dry to quite sweet. Sweet sherry is often called cream sherry, as in Harvey's Bristol Cream. Really good sherry is made in Spain by British companies who export it all over the world. The Chinese love it in sauces and soups, and it does add a wonderful flavor. It's also good in shrimp bisque, lobster Newburg, and other seafood dishes.

Makes 2½ cups

3 tablespoons unsalted butter
3 tablespoons corn flour
2 cups milk or cream, warmed
⅔ cup grated sharp Cheddar cheese
¼ cup minced GF smoked ham
2 teaspoons sherry
Salt and pure black pepper to taste

Rich Cream Sauce with Prosciutto, Gorgonzola, and Walnuts

Makes 2½ cups

3 tablespoons unsalted butter
3 tablespoons corn flour
2 cups medium cream, warmed
2 tablespoons minced GF prosciutto ham
½ cup crumbled Gorgonzola or blue cheese
¼ teaspoon ground nutmeg
½ cup walnut pieces, toasted
Salt and pure black pepper to taste

This is still another delicious variation on the basic cream sauce.

1. Melt the butter and stir in the flour. Sauté, stirring for 4 to 5 minutes over medium-low heat. Add the warm cream, whisking constantly until thickened to desired consistency.

2. Remove from the heat and stir in the prosciutto, cheese, nutmeg, walnuts, and salt and pepper. Serve immediately.

Rich Cream Sauces Are Versatile

You can add herbs, stock, or even GF bacon to a rich cream sauce. You can add cheese such as mascarpone or some GF prosciutto ham. The addition of mushrooms adds body and flavor too. You can adapt cream sauce to loads of fish, meat, and vegetable dishes and benefit from the lush flavors.

Basic Aioli (French or Italian Mayonnaise)

This is so much tastier than commercial mayonnaise from a jar. Use room-temperature eggs or the aioli will be too thin.

1. Place the eggs, garlic, mustard, and lemon juice or vinegar in the jar of an electric blender. Blend vigorously.

2. Turn motor to low and very slowly add the oils, salt, and pepper. Refrigerate in a closed container. (Some variations you can try include adding ½ teaspoon GF anchovy paste, or to taste; lemon zest; various herbs; coriander seed; anise seed; GF chili sauce; or chopped fresh fennel.)

The Mother of Mayonnaise

Aioli and mayonnaise are made with basically the same ingredients, with one exception: aioli has a lot of garlic flavor in it. It is loaded with character and can be spooned into Mediterranean seafood stews and soups or spread on gluten-free bread and sprinkled with cheese for a tasty crouton. Drop spoonfuls in soups or serve with seafood as a dressing.

Makes 1½ cups

2 eggs at room temperature
2 cloves garlic
1 teaspoon GF English
    mustard
1 tablespoon fresh lemon juice
    or white wine vinegar
½ cup olive oil
½ cup canola oil
Salt and pure black pepper
    to taste

Creamy Mushroom and Cognac Sauce

Serves 4

½ cup cognac
1 4-ounce package dried
 porcini or Asian black
 mushrooms
3 tablespoons unsalted butter
3 tablespoons chestnut flour
4 shallots, minced
10 ounces button mushrooms,
 bases of stems removed
¼ teaspoon nutmeg
1 cup GF beef broth
1 cup heavy cream
1 tablespoon fresh thyme
Salt and freshly ground black
 pepper to taste

This goes great over gluten-free pasta, polenta, or rice. Add an extra 1½ cups of GF broth to the recipe to turn it into soup.

1. Place the cognac and dried mushrooms in a saucepan and add water to cover. Simmer over low heat for 10 minutes. Remove from the stove and cool. Puree in the blender until very smooth.

2. Melt the butter and stir in the chestnut flour, stirring until well blended. Add the shallots and button mushrooms, stirring constantly. Whisk in the rest of the ingredients, including the pureed mushroom-and-cognac mixture. (At this point you can add 1½ cups extra broth to make soup.)

A Simple Staple

Polenta is a staple in Italy and it's hard to ruin it. You can use polenta wherever you'd use pasta, serving it with tomato, vegetable, or cream sauces, or with brown gravy with mushrooms. You can make it soft, to mound on a plate or platter, or firm and then fry it in squares.

Ham, Broccoli, and Shrimp Pasta Sauce

This is excellent over Asian rice noodles. You can substitute chicken strips for the shrimp.

1. Bring a pot of salted water to a boil. Drop the broccoli into the boiling water and cook for 10 minutes. Drain and set aside.

2. Heat the oils and add the garlic; do not brown. Stir in the ham.

3. Add the broccoli and the rest of the ingredients, except for the pine nuts and cilantro. The dish is done when the shrimp turn pink. Garnish with pine nuts and chopped cilantro or parsley and serve.

Serves 4

1 head broccoli, stems removed, divided into small florets
2 tablespoons olive oil
1 teaspoon sesame oil
2 cloves garlic, thinly sliced
4 ounces GF smoked ham, finely chopped
Juice of ½ lemon
½ cup dry white wine
2 tablespoons GF soy sauce or GF Worcestershire sauce
1 pound raw shrimp, peeled and deveined
1 teaspoon sugar
½ cup toasted pine nuts and ¼ cup chopped cilantro or parsley to garnish

Spicy Spinach and Lobster Sauce

Serves 4

1 1½-pound lobster
2 tablespoons butter
2 tablespoons cornstarch
1 cup hot GF chicken or clam broth
1 cup heavy cream
3 cups fresh baby spinach, rinsed and stems trimmed
1 tablespoon dry sherry
Pinch ground nutmeg
1 teaspoon pure hot red pepper flakes or cayenne pepper
Salt and pure black pepper to taste

Quinoa pasta is high in protein and can be used as you would almost any pasta. Rice pasta is found in Asian markets and some supermarkets.

1. Plunge the lobster into plenty of boiling salted water. Cook for 15 minutes. Cool; crack the shell and remove the meat. Set the meat aside.

2. Melt the butter and add the cornstarch, stirring until smooth. Whisk in the chicken broth. Add the cream and heat.

3. Stir in the spinach and cook until wilted. Add the sherry, nutmeg, red pepper flakes, and reserved lobster. Sprinkle with salt and pepper. Serve over quinoa or rice pasta.

Greek Eggplant and Olive Sauce

Here you have many of the flavors of Greece without the travel. Touches of garlic and mint do not overwhelm. Goes great over pasta or rice.

1. Dredge the eggplant cubes in flour and salt. In a saucepan, heat the olive oil over medium-high heat. Sauté the eggplant until brown.

2. When brown, lower heat and add the garlic; sauté for another 3 minutes.

3. Add the rest of the ingredients and serve.

Serves 4

1 medium eggplant, peeled and cubed
½ cup rice flour mixed with 1 teaspoon salt
⅓ cup olive oil
2 cloves garlic, minced
½ cup kalamata or other black Greek olives, pitted and chopped
10 mint leaves, coarsely chopped
½ cup finely snipped chives
Juice of ½ lemon
Extra olive oil if sauce seems dry

Confetti and Rice Pasta with Chicken

Serves 4

½ cup olive oil

½ cup finely chopped sweet red pepper

½ cup finely chopped yellow summer squash

1 bunch scallions, chopped fine

2 cloves garlic, chopped fine

½ cup rice or corn flour

1 teaspoon salt

½ teaspoon pure black pepper, or to taste

½ teaspoon dried thyme

¾ pound boneless, skinless chicken breast, cut into bite-sized pieces

½ cup GF chicken broth

8 ripe plum (Roma) tomatoes, chopped, or 1½ cups canned (GF)

1 teaspoon dried oregano

1 teaspoon dried basil

1 tablespoon pure red pepper flakes, or to taste

1 pound rice pasta, cooked (check that it is free of wheat)

1 cup freshly grated Parmesan cheese

This is fun to eat and pretty to look at. The "confetti" is minced vegetables. Lots of Parmesan cheese completes the dish.

1. Heat the olive oil and add the pepper, squash, scallions, and garlic. Sauté over medium heat, stirring frequently. While the vegetables are sautéing, mix the flour, salt, pepper, and thyme on a piece of waxed paper.

2. Dredge the chicken in the flour mixture and sauté along with the vegetables. Add the broth, tomatoes, oregano, basil, and plenty of red pepper flakes. Cook, uncovered, for 10 minutes to make sure the chicken is done.

3. Add the rice pasta to the pan of sauce and mix. Sprinkle with plenty of Parmesan cheese and serve.

Rice Pasta

Rice pasta is available online and at Asian markets. Many supermarkets also carry it. Soba—Japanese noodles—have both buckwheat flour and wheat flour in them, and sometimes the contents are listed in Japanese characters. Although it is "rice" pasta, check ingredients for gluten offenders such as wheat!

Hazelnut, Sour Cream, and Ham Sauce

This is so rich, you don't need much. It's a very good side dish with seafood, fish, or chicken.

1. Cook the pasta according to package directions. Chop the nuts coarsely in your food processor.

2. While the pasta is cooking, sauté the shallots in olive oil. When soft, about 5 minutes, add the toasted hazelnuts, ham, and sour cream.

3. Turn heat down to warm, and as soon as sour cream is hot, sprinkle with pepper and celery salt and serve.

Hazelnuts, Ready to Use

Hazelnuts have hard shells, and after you crack them and get the meat out, you have to skin them. Recently, ready-to-use hazelnuts have become available in stores. How sweet it is to find them all ready to go in a plastic container. They toast up nicely for use in salads, or you can grind them or chop them to crust a piece of fish or a boneless duck breast.

Serves 4 as a side dish

½ pound GF pasta
1 cup hazelnuts, toasted and peeled
4 shallots, minced
¼ cup olive oil
1 cup finely diced GF Virginia ham
1½ cups GF sour cream (not low-fat)
Freshly ground black pepper and celery salt

Green Tomato (Tomatillo) Salsa
Spicy Tomato Salsa
Apple, Cranberry, and Walnut Chutney
Mango, Cherry, and Apricot Chutney
Tropical Fruit Salsa
Sweet and Hot Pineapple Salsa
Green Sauce
Mango Salsa
Curry-Mustard Mayonnaise
Classic Red Tomato Salsa
Incredible Hollandaise Sauce
Sauce Maltaise
Sauce Béarnaise
Sweet and Tart Whipped Prune and Brandy Sauce
White and Red Grape Sauce for Poultry and Game
Currant and Port Sauce for Pork or Game
Pesto with Mint
Pesto Sauce
Sweet and Hot Yellow Tomato Coulis
Sweet Red Pepper Sauce
Zucchini Sauce for Seafood
Roasted Garlic Sauce with Cream and Cheese
Caper Sauce for Fish, Meat, or Poultry
White Wine Sauce
Red Wine Sauce

Dressings

chapter twelve

Green Tomato (Tomatillo) Salsa

Makes about 1 cup

10–12 tomatillos, husked, rinsed, and chopped
2 tablespoons olive oil
1 yellow tomato, cored and chopped fine
½ red onion, chopped fine
2 cloves garlic, minced
Juice of 1 lime and ½ teaspoon lime zest
2 serrano chilies, cored, seeded, and minced
1 teaspoon salt, or to taste
¼ cup minced parsley or cilantro

Tomatillos are small green-tomato-like fruit with papery husks. They are available in many supermarkets and all Latino markets.

Combine all ingredients in a bowl and cover. Let stand for 2 hours or refrigerate overnight. Serve at room temperature.

Spicy Tomato Salsa

Salsa made with fresh tomatoes and herbs is such a treat. Of course, you can vary it tremendously. Have fun with it, adding extras from your garden.

Mix all ingredients in a food processor, pulsing until coarsely chopped. Refrigerate until ready to serve.

Makes about 1½ cups

10 large, fresh plum or Roma tomatoes, blanched in boiling water, skinned
¼ cup lemon juice
3 cloves garlic, minced
2 ears cooked corn, kernels cut from the cob
1 teaspoon cumin
2 onions, peeled, cut into quarters
Salt and GF hot pepper sauce to taste
½ cup chopped fresh cilantro or parsley, to taste

Apple, Cranberry, and Walnut Chutney

Makes 2 cups

½ cup finely chopped shallots
2 tablespoons cooking oil
2 cups cranberries, fresh or frozen, washed and picked over if fresh
2 tart apples, peeled, cored, and chopped
½ cup brown sugar, or to taste
¼ cup cider vinegar
2 ounces water
1 teaspoon orange zest
½ teaspoon ground coriander seed
½ teaspoon pure black pepper
½ teaspoon salt
½ cup walnut pieces, toasted

This is excellent with duckling, chicken, and, of course, turkey. It's easy to make and will keep for 2 weeks in the refrigerator. Or make a lot and freeze it.

1. Cook the shallots in oil until softened in a large, heavy saucepan.

2. Mix everything but the walnuts in with the shallots. Cook, stirring, until berries have popped and the sauce has become very thick.

3. Cool and stir in toasted walnut pieces. Store in the refrigerator.

Fruit and Pepper

Try putting some pepper on watermelon, cantaloupe, or honeydew melon. You'll find that peppery chutneys and GF salsas make an excellent accompaniment to all kinds of dishes.

Mango, Cherry, and Apricot Chutney

Make a double recipe—it's so good, you'll want more. It's wonderful with swordfish and shrimp.

Combine all ingredients in a bowl and mix well. Cover and refrigerate overnight. Serve at room temperature. (This will keep for 2 to 3 days in the fridge.)

Ginger Root

Although ginger root, a true spice, is wonderful in Asian dishes, it's also very good in beef and lamb stews. Grandmothers used to crumble up ginger snaps to add to stews and stuffings. Ginger keeps well in the refrigerator or freezer, and all you have to do is break off a chunk, peel it, and chop it. Dried ginger root is also available, but fresh is so much better.

Makes 1½ cups

2 ripe mangos, peeled and chopped
½ cup dried cherries soaked in ½ cup hot water
2–3 ripe apricots, blanched, peeled, halved, and pitted
1 jalapeño chili, cored, seeded, and minced
1 tablespoon minced fresh ginger root
1 tablespoon brown sugar, or to taste
2 shallots, chopped
Juice of 1 large lemon

Tropical Fruit Salsa

Makes about 1½ cups

1 large mango, peeled, seeded, and diced
1 cup fresh pineapple, diced
¼ cup minced red onion
1 teaspoon Tabasco sauce, or to taste
½ teaspoon freshly grated lime zest
Juice of ½ lime
Salt to taste

The sweet-hot combination is wonderful. Try it with pork, lamb, or any kind of fish.

Mix all ingredients in a bowl and cover. Refrigerate for 2 hours. Serve at room temperature.

Chilies—Handle with Care

When handling chilies, it's very wise to wear rubber gloves. If they burn your mouth, they can also burn your skin. If you do not use gloves, be sure to wash your hands immediately and thoroughly after handling chilies. And be careful with them. Anything punishingly hot will kill taste buds, so you will need more and more heat over time to taste it at all.

Sweet and Hot Pineapple Salsa

This is delicious any time of year.

Mix all ingredients in food processor and pulse until coarsely chopped. Vary with chopped, toasted nuts, and/or crisp bits of apple or jicama.

Food Processor Sense

Today, you can buy small, medium, or large food processors. To prevent mess, process your food in batches. Otherwise, the liquid or soupy stuff will spill out and make a mess of your machine and your countertop.

Makes 2 cups

1½ cups fresh pineapple chunks
2 tablespoons brown sugar
1 tablespoon GF hot pepper sauce
¼ cup fresh lemon juice
Salt to taste
½ teaspoon ground coriander
½ cup chopped sweet red onion

Green Sauce

Makes 1½ cups

1½ cups commercial GF
    mayonnaise
¼ cup snipped fresh dill weed
½ cup chopped fresh parsley
6 fresh basil leaves, torn
1 teaspoon coarsely ground
    pure black pepper
Lemon juice (optional)

This is another versatile sauce, wonderful over seafood or vegetables or chicken.

1. Whirl all ingredients in blender or food processor.

2. Store in the refrigerator.

Green Sauce for Salmon

Green sauce is popular with salmon. It can be made with different herbs, GF mayonnaise, and lemon juice. The point is to use lots of fresh green herbs to give it that great color and flavor.

Mango Salsa

This is quick and easy. Try it with cold chicken, seafood, or grilled fish.

Mix all ingredients together and let stand for 2 hours or in the fridge overnight. Serve at room temperature or cold.

Makes about 1 cup

2 ripe mangos, peeled, seeded, and chopped
1 jalapeño chili, or to taste, minced
Juice of 1 lime
1 teaspoon lime zest
2 tablespoons minced red onion
1 teaspoon sugar
Salt to taste
¼ cup chopped fresh mint or parsley

Curry-Mustard Mayonnaise

Makes 1½ cups

1 recipe Basic Aioli (see page 179) or 1½ cups commercial GF mayonnaise
2 teaspoons GF curry powder, or to taste
2 teaspoons GF Dijon mustard, or to taste
1 tablespoon lemon juice
Dash Tabasco

This is fabulous in a rice salad with seafood or chicken. It's also excellent with grilled vegetables.

Whisk all ingredients together in a bowl, cover, and refrigerate. Variations include adding herbs, green peppercorns, or capers.

Curry-Mustard Sauce

This is excellent on all kinds of cold meats and in rice salads. A classic use of curry-mustard mayonnaise is in the French recipe for chicken salad Boulestin, with chunks of chicken and rice. It is also good in a rice-and-vegetable salad. Try it also as a dipping sauce for shrimp.

Classic Red Tomato Salsa

Your own homemade salsa with red, ripe tomatoes tastes so much better than jarred!

1. Put all ingredients in a food processor and pulse until well blended. Do not puree.

2. Serve after 1 hour or refrigerate overnight. You can vary the amount of chilies to taste.

Salsa Style

Salsa is a Mexican invention, using the hot and sweet peppers, tomatoes, herbs, and spices available. Hot food has a purpose in a hot climate: it makes you sweat, and when you sweat, you cool off—a bit. Foods that are extremely hot do kill taste buds, so don't punish your mouth.

Makes 1½ to 2 cups

6 large, ripe, juicy red tomatoes
2 cloves garlic
2 serrano or jalapeño chilies, or to taste, cored, seeded, and chopped
½ cup minced sweet white onion
Juice of 1 lime
1 teaspoon salt, or to taste
½ cup minced cilantro

Incredible Hollandaise Sauce

Makes 1¼ cups

2 sticks (1 cup) unsalted butter
1 whole egg and 1 or 2 egg yolks, depending on the richness desired
1 tablespoon freshly squeezed lemon juice
⅛ teaspoon cayenne pepper
Salt to taste

This sauce can be varied enormously. It's perfect on fish, lobster, or hot vegetables, especially asparagus, artichokes, and broccoli.

1. Melt the butter in a small, heavy saucepan over very low heat. Put the eggs, lemon juice, and cayenne in the jar of a blender or food processor. Blend well.

2. With the motor running on low, add the hot butter, a little at a time, to the egg mixture.

3. Return to the pan you used to melt the butter. Whisking, thicken the sauce over low heat, adding salt. As soon as thick, pour into a bowl, a sauce boat, or over the food. (Reheating the sauce to thicken it is the delicate stage. You must not let it get too hot or it will scramble the eggs, or even curdle them. If either disaster happens, add a tablespoon of boiling water and whisk like mad.)

Hollandaise Sauce

The name implies that this sauce was created in Holland, a land of high butter use. However, it is not called Holland sauce; we get a French spelling. In any area where there is plentiful butter, hollandaise sauce, with its rich, smooth texture, will reign. And although people tend to think of it in terms of eggs Benedict, it's good on most green vegetables.

Sauce Maltaise

This is a wonderful variation on hollandaise sauce that is perfect with fish, seafood,
chicken, or vegetables.

1. Melt the butter in a small, heavy saucepan
over very low heat. Put the eggs, orange juice,
orange zest, salt, and cayenne in the jar of a
blender or food processor. Blend well. Season
to taste and add Tabasco if desired.

2. With the motor running on low, add the hot
butter, a little at a time, to the egg mixture.

3. Return to the pan you used to melt the
butter. Whisking, thicken the sauce over low
heat, and as soon as thick, pour into a bowl, a
sauce boat, or over the food. (Reheating the
sauce to thicken it is the delicate stage. You
must not let it get too hot or it will scramble
the eggs, or even curdle them. If either disaster happens, add a tablespoon of boiling water
and whisk like mad.) Serve immediately.

Makes 1 cup

2 sticks (1 cup) unsalted
    butter
1 whole egg and 1 or 2 egg
    yolks, depending on the
    richness desired
1 tablespoon freshly squeezed
    orange juice
½ teaspoon orange zest
⅛ teaspoon cayenne pepper
Salt to taste
Tabasco sauce to taste
    (optional)

Sauce Béarnaise

Makes 1¼ cups

2 sticks (1 cup) unsalted
    butter
1 whole egg and 1 or 2 egg
    yolks, depending on the
    richness desired
1 tablespoon white wine
    vinegar
½ teaspoon dried tarragon
⅛ teaspoon cayenne pepper
Salt to taste

This classic sauce is usually served with filet mignon, prime rib of beef, or fish. It's excellent with swordfish or salmon.

1. Melt the butter in a small, heavy saucepan over very low heat. Put the eggs, vinegar, tarragon, and cayenne in the jar of a blender or food processor. Blend well.

2. With the motor running on low, add the hot butter, a little at a time, to the egg mixture.

3. Return to the pan you used to melt the butter. Add salt. Whisking, thicken the sauce over low heat, and as soon as thick, pour into a bowl, a sauce boat, or over the food. (Reheating the sauce to thicken it is the delicate stage. You must not let it get too hot or it will scramble the eggs, or even curdle them. If either disaster happens, add a tablespoon of boiling water and whisk like mad.)

Sweet and Tart Whipped Prune and Brandy Sauce

This is a natural with game. It's also wonderful with turkey and pork. Just put a tablespoonful over whatever you've fixed and it's great.

1. Soak the prunes in the brandy until they are plump. Whirl the prune/brandy mixture with the allspice in the blender and set aside.

2. Whip the cream with the pepper until stiff.

3. Warm the brandy/prune mixture, fold in whipped cream, and serve as a condiment.

Brandy as a Spice and Flavoring

Adding brandy to a sauce or stew will give you a wonderful nutty nuance. The alcohol cooks away and evaporates. Don't worry—no one will get tipsy on a brandy sauce. When it's added to a brown gravy or a cream sauce, it's sublime.

Makes 1 cup

½ cup pitted prunes
½ cup cognac or brandy
¼ teaspoon allspice
½ cup heavy cream
¼ teaspoon ground pure black
   pepper

White and Red Grape Sauce for Poultry and Game

Makes 2 cups

2 tablespoons unsalted butter
2 shallots, chopped
2 tablespoons cornstarch
1 cup GF chicken broth, warmed
½ cup seedless red grapes, washed and halved
½ cup seedless green grapes, washed and halved
¼ cup dry white wine
1 teaspoon rosemary leaves
10 fresh basil leaves
1 teaspoon GF Worcestershire sauce
Salt and pure black pepper to taste

This is wonderful with chicken, turkey, or duck. For an exciting taste, try it with bison or venison.

1. Melt the butter and sauté the shallots. When they are soft, after about 5 minutes over medium heat, stir in cornstarch; cook for 4 minutes. Whisk in the warm broth and add the grapes, wine, and herbs. (For a variation, you can add half a cup of heavy cream or some lemon juice.) Bring to a boil and cook for 10 minutes, until grapes are softened.

2. Add the Worcestershire, salt, and pepper. Serve hot.

Chutney

The British fell in love with chutney when they ruled India. You can buy basic chutneys in the supermarket; however, a good Indian cook will make chutney especially to go with what he or she is serving. It's wonderful with any cold meat or hot curries.

Currant and Port Sauce for Pork or Game

A little goes a long way, so it's best to serve it in a sauce boat on the side so people can take as much or as little as they please.

1. Heat the jelly and port in a saucepan. Mix the water and cornstarch together and whisk it into the jelly/port mixture. Boil for 5 minutes.

2. Add the rest of the ingredients and serve. (For variations, you can add 1 tablespoon fresh orange juice, 1 teaspoon lemon juice, or ¼ cup heavy cream.)

Au "Currant"

Currants are small berries that grow on bushes. They have a nice tart bite to them, but when dried, they taste quite sweet. Currant jelly is readily available and classically served with game birds and venison. Currant jelly is also an excellent condiment for turkey, as an alternative to cranberry sauce.

Makes about 1 cup

½ cup currant jelly
½ cup port wine
¼ cup water
2 teaspoons cornstarch
⅛ teaspoon ground cloves
⅛ teaspoon ground allspice
½ teaspoon salt
Freshly ground pure black
pepper to taste

Pesto with Mint

Makes abut 1 cup

½ cup fresh mint, washed and
  patted dry on paper towels
½ cup fresh Italian flat-leaf
  parsley, rinsed and patted
  dry
¾ cup extra-virgin olive oil,
  more if needed
Juice of ½ fresh lemon
½ teaspoon pure black pepper
½ cup blanched almonds,
  toasted
Salt to taste

This is great with lamb, pork, and any vegetables.

Whirl all ingredients in a blender. Taste before
adding extra salt.

More Mints Than Can Be Imagined

Take a stroll through a big herb farm and you
will see myriad varieties of mint. Aside from
spearmint and peppermint, there is orange
mint, lemon mint, and even chocolate mint.
Mint grows like a weed and can take over a
garden with little encouragement. Plant the
seedlings in a coffee can that you've removed
the lid and bottom from to make a hollow cylin-
der. Then the mint won't send out runners and
spread—too much.

Pesto Sauce

This is a classic sauce. It's great with vegetables and spaghetti squash, fine over rice noodles.

Place all ingredients in blender and whirl until pureed. You may need to add a bit of extra olive oil if it seems too dry. Serve immediately.

Spaghetti Squash, the "Almost" Pasta

We found that we like spaghetti squash as much as pasta. It adapts to any sauce that you would make for gluten-heavy pasta. Use it freely with GF Bolognese, Alfredo, carbonara, seafood sauces, and just plain old GF tomato sauce. For a simple side, it's excellent dressed with butter, Parmesan cheese, and fresh herbs.

Makes 1½ cups

2 cups fresh basil leaves, rinsed, patted dry, and packed
2–3 cloves fresh garlic
1 cup extra-virgin olive oil
½ cup pine nuts, toasted
Salt and pure black pepper to taste

Sweet and Hot
Yellow Tomato Coulis

Make 1½ cups

4 large yellow tomatoes,
   rinsed, cored, and chopped
2 cloves garlic, halved
3 shallots, cut up
½ cup extra-virgin olive oil
1 tablespoon orange juice
1 tablespoon finely chopped
   parsley
Salt and pure black pepper
   to taste

This is excellent drizzled over shrimp, fish, or poultry. Its fresh taste will keep in the refrigerator or freezer.

Put all ingredients in blender. Puree. Serve cold, or warm the sauce over low heat.

Tomatoes

Yellow tomatoes are much sweeter than red ones. They are great fried, cooked into sauce, or made into a coulis. The only trouble with yellow tomatoes is that they have a short season. When you see them, whether large or cherry-tomato size, get them, and start eating them out of hand. Or serve them with some fresh basil and a drizzle of olive oil.

Sweet Red Pepper Sauce

This takes only a minute or two to prepare—time well spent. Spoon over grilled vegetables, soups, pork, or chicken. You can also use it as a dip with chips.

1. Whirl the roasted peppers, garlic, lemon juice, and basil in a blender, then pour into a bowl.

2. Whisk in the sour cream, then add salt and pepper. Serve chilled.

Makes 1 cup

½ cup roasted red peppers
    packed in oil
1 clove garlic
2 tablespoons lemon juice
4 fresh basil leaves
½ cup GF sour cream
Salt and pure black pepper
    to taste

Zucchini Sauce for Seafood

Makes 1½ cups

1 cup steamed zucchini
2 cloves garlic
¼ cup GF chicken broth
2 tablespoons minced shallot
2 tablespoons lime juice
¼ cup olive oil
Salt and Tabasco sauce to
    taste

This is excellent with grilled shrimp, scallops, or poultry.

Put all ingredients in a blender. Puree. Serve warm or cold.

Making Interesting Sauces and Coulis

When you puree such vegetables as roasted red peppers and cooked summer squash and zucchini, you get a nice, creamy base for flavors. Add your favorite herbs and fresh lemon, lime, or orange juice. You can adjust the heat to your personal taste. You can also add cream, GF sour cream, or GF mayonnaise for extra smoothness.

Roasted Garlic Sauce with Cream and Cheese

Roasting garlic changes its flavor. It becomes milder, softer, and sweeter.

1. Preheat oven to 300°F.

2. Wrap the dampened garlic in aluminum foil and roast in oven for 60 minutes. Cool until you can handle it. Cut off the tip ends and squeeze garlic out of the shells; set aside.

3. Melt butter over low heat and stir in the cornstarch. Continue to cook for a few minutes over low heat. Whisk in chicken broth, parsley, and olive oil.

4. Add vinegar or lemon juice, salt, pepper, and cheese. Whirl all ingredients in the blender. Pour into a serving bowl and use with vegetables, spaghetti squash, salads, rice, or tomatoes.

Makes ¾ cup

1 head garlic unpeeled, dampened
3 teaspoons unsalted butter
1 teaspoon cornstarch
¼ cup GF chicken broth
2 tablespoons minced Italian flat-leaf parsley
2 tablespoons olive oil
1 teaspoon vinegar or lemon juice
Salt and pure black pepper to taste
2 tablespoons Parmesan cheese
½ cup heavy cream

Caper Sauce for Fish, Meat, or Poultry

Makes ½ cup

4 tablespoons unsalted butter
1 tablespoon extra-virgin
   olive oil
2 large shallots, chopped
1 clove garlic, chopped
3 tablespoons capers
¼ cup dry white wine
1 teaspoon lemon juice
½ cup chopped parsley
4 mint leaves, shredded
Salt and pure black pepper
   to taste

These Mediterranean ingredients will sauce any number of entrées. You can use this on most dishes as sauce and/or flavoring.

1. Heat butter, olive oil, and shallots in a saucepan and sauté, stirring for 5 minutes.

2. Add the rest of the ingredients and cook, stirring, for another 5 minutes. Pour over your entree, fish, poultry, steak, or grilled vegetables.

Shallots

Shallots are both sweet and aromatic. Try roasting them, or caramelizing them in a pan with a bit of butter. They are part of the onion family, but a gentle part. They are milder than onions, and some people think they have a garlicky flavor. They are quite versatile.

White Wine Sauce

You can vary the herbs or add some sliced mushrooms, olives, capers, or green peppercorns. Pour the sauce over any fish or meat, mashed potatoes, or rice.

1. Sauté the onion for 4 minutes in the butter and oil. Whisk in the cornstarch and cook for 3 to 4 minutes.

2. Whisk in the warm chicken broth, stirring until smooth. Then add the wine or vermouth. Swirl in the mustard, herbs, salt, and pepper. Simmer over low heat for 10 minutes, stirring occasionally.

3. Add cream if desired. Serve hot.

Makes 1½ cups

½ cup minced sweet onion
2 tablespoons unsalted butter
1 tablespoon extra-virgin olive oil
3 tablespoons cornstarch
1 cup GF chicken broth, warmed
½ cup dry white wine or white vermouth
½ teaspoon prepared GF Dijon mustard
¼ cup chopped parsley
1 teaspoon shredded fresh basil
½ teaspoon dried tarragon or rosemary
Salt and pure black pepper to taste
½ cup heavy cream (optional)

Red Wine Sauce

Makes 2 cups

4 shallots, peeled and
   chopped fine
2 cloves garlic, or to taste,
   minced
2 tablespoons butter
2 tablespoons olive oil
1 cup sliced mushrooms,
   brown, white button, or
   exotic
3 teaspoons potato, corn, or
   rice flour
1 cup GF beef broth, heated
1 cup dry red wine such as
   Burgundy or Merlot
1 tablespoon GF Worcestershire sauce
Salt and pure black pepper
   to taste

Once you've had this with filet mignon, prime rib, or an elegant hamburger, you'll make it often.

1. Sauté the shallots and garlic in butter and oil in a large saucepan over low heat. Toss the mushrooms to coat in the butter and oil. Blend in the flour and simmer for 10 minutes, stirring.

2. Whisk in the broth and red wine, Worcestershire, salt, and pepper. Bring to a boil. Reduce heat and simmer over very low heat for 20 minutes.

Variations on a Theme

There are many, many different variations to this recipe. There is much to love about this very simple and basic sauce—that's why it's been popular for more than 200 years. Try different herbs such as parsley, rosemary, or basil. You can add heat using a few drops of GF hot red pepper sauce such as Tabasco. Capers, chopped olives, or green peppercorns also can add a nice touch.

Popcorn with Spicy Butter

Roasted Pink Pepper Nuts

Crunchy Cornbread Squares

Chili Bean Dip with Dipping Vegetables

Hot and Sweet Peppers with
Jack Cheese Stuffing

Peppers with Jalapeño Jelly and
Cream Cheese Stuffing

Deviled Eggs with Caviar or Shrimp

Grilled Curried Chicken Wings

Grilled Hot-to-Eight-Alarm Chicken Wings

Stuffed Celery with Gorgonzola
and Green Peppercorns

Baby Back Ribs

Grilled Cheese on Toasted Cornbread Squares

Chickpea Crepes for Stuffing

Hot Hot Dogs

Curried Chicken

Peanut Butter, Banana, and Bacon Stuffing

Pepperoni and Cheese Stuffing

Snacks

chapter thirteen

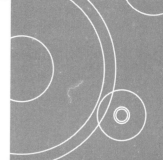

Popcorn with
Spicy Butter

Serves 2

½ stick (¼ cup) butter or
 margarine
1 teaspoon Tabasco sauce
½ teaspoon freshly ground
 black pepper
1 teaspoon salt
1 package plain microwave
 popcorn or 4 cups popped
 corn, unflavored and unbut-
 tered

This is an excellent change from regular buttered popcorn. You can add more heat to it if
you like, as well as seasoned salt.

Melt the butter and add seasonings. Pour over
hot popcorn, mixing vigorously.

Roasted Pink Pepper Nuts

These will keep in a tight plastic or tin container. You can also substitute black or white pepper with only slightly different results.

1. Preheat oven to 350°F. Line a cookie sheet with aluminum foil and treat with GF nonstick spray.

2. Melt the butter and add sugar and water. Mix, stirring over medium heat. Add the spices, salt, and pepper. When well blended, add the almonds and coat.

3. Transfer the nuts to the cookie sheet. Bake for about 10 minutes, until well browned. Cool and store in airtight container.

Makes 2½ cups

½ stick (¼ cup) unsalted butter
¾ cup golden brown sugar (not "brownulated")
4 teaspoons water
½ teaspoon ground cloves
¼ teaspoon cinnamon
2 teaspoons salt
1 tablespoon freshly ground pink peppercorns
2½ cups blanched almonds

Crunchy Cornbread Squares

Makes 15 to 20 squares

1 cup cornmeal
1 cup corn flour
2 teaspoons baking soda
1 teaspoon cream of tartar
1 teaspoon salt, or to taste
4 tablespoons white or brown
    sugar
1 cup GF sour cream
¼ cup buttermilk
2 beaten eggs
4 tablespoons butter, melted

These can also be cut into rectangles and used as bases for dips and spreads.

1. Prepare a 9" x 13" baking pan with GF non-stick spray and preheat oven to 425°F. Mix all of the dry ingredients together in a bowl. Stir in sour cream, buttermilk, and eggs. (You can add various herbs and spices to change the flavors, such as oregano and garlic powder for an Italian flavor, or chili and cumin for a Mexican taste.)

2. Pour into the prepared baking pan and bake for 20 minutes or until lightly browned.

Snacking

Always a part of American eating habits, snacks should be a healthful addition to the diet. Overly sweet snacks such as cakes and candies are not all that helpful, as they produce a sugar high followed by more hunger. Real food is satisfying and keeps away hunger.

Chili Bean Dip
with Dipping Vegetables

This is a great addition to any snack tray, whether for watching a game on TV or after school.

1. Sauté the beef and vegetables in the oil, breaking up with a spoon to avoid clumping.

2. When the vegetables are soft, add the rest of the ingredients (except the vegetables for dipping). Cover and simmer for 1 hour. Serve warm, or cool and turn into a dip by pulsing it in the food processor. Do not make it smooth. Serve alongside veggies.

Chili and Beans

There are endless variations of the chili-and-bean combination. Some people use turkey, others add dark chocolate and cinnamon and vary the amounts of beans and tomatoes. Some forms of chili don't have any beans. Various regions use various amounts of spice, heat, and ingredients.

Makes 1 quart

½ pound ground beef
1 onion, chopped
2 jalapeño peppers, or to taste, cored, seeded, and chopped
2 cloves garlic, chopped
¼ cup vegetable oil
4 teaspoons GF chili powder, or to taste
1 13-ounce can GF crushed tomatoes with juice
1 13-ounce can red kidney beans
½ cup flat GF beer
Assortment of carrots, celery pieces, radishes, broccoli, spears of zucchini, etc.

Hot and Sweet Peppers with Jack Cheese Stuffing

Serves 4

4 sweet red bell peppers, cut in quarters, cored, and seeded

4 teaspoons olive oil, or spray bottle of olive oil

4 ounces Monterey jack or pepper jack cheese, shredded

½ cup Crunchy Cornbread Squares (see page 216), crumbled in the blender or food processor

Freshly ground black pepper and cayenne to taste

4 teaspoons Parmesan cheese for topping

Shredded lettuce and GF sour cream, for garnish

This is an easy snack or cocktail nibble.

1. Preheat oven to 350°F.

2. Prepare a baking dish with GF nonstick spray. Lay the peppers in the dish. Spray or drizzle them with olive oil. Divide the jack cheese between the peppers.

3. Mix the crumbs, pepper, cayenne, and Parmesan together and spoon over the jack cheese in the peppers. Bake until the cheese melts, about 10 minutes. Serve garnished with shredded lettuce and a dollop of sour cream.

Peppers with Jalapeño Jelly and Cream Cheese Stuffing

This can also be served on GF crackers or Crunchy Cornbread Squares (see page 216). The combination of sweet, hot, and creamy is irresistible.

Arrange the cut pepper "spoons" on a platter. Place a dab of cream cheese on each, add a dab of the hot/sweet jalapeño jelly, and serve.

Makes 32 pieces

4 large, ripe, red bell peppers, cored, seeded, cut into quarters, and then halved
1 8-ounce package cream cheese
1 8-ounce jar jalapeño jelly

Deviled Eggs
with Caviar or Shrimp

Make 10 deviled eggs

5 hard-boiled eggs
½ cup whole or low-fat GF mayonnaise
1 teaspoon GF Dijon mustard
1 teaspoon Tabasco sauce or other GF hot red pepper sauce
½ bunch of chives, snipped finely
2 teaspoons capers, the smallest available
2 ounces GF red salmon caviar or 10 small cooked shrimp
GF sour cream if you are using caviar

There is nothing more delightful than a deviled egg with a dab of caviar on top and a dab of GF sour cream on top of that.

1. Peel eggs, cut them in half, and remove the yolks to your food processor. Arrange the whites on the platter.

2. Add the mayonnaise, mustard, pepper sauce, chives, and capers to the food processor and whirl until blended.

3. Stuff the egg whites with the yolk mixture and place ¼ teaspoon caviar or a small shrimp on top of each. Serve with sour cream on the side to go with the caviar.

Olive Oil in Spray Bottles

This is a very easy and economical way to use olive oil. Just buy a bottle used for spraying plants with water and fill it with olive oil. Use it for spraying your food, salads, et cetera. Or you can get olive oil–flavored GF nonstick spray at the supermarket. The GF nonstick spray, however, is not suitable for salads.

Grilled Curried Chicken Wings

Traditional buffalo wings are generally fried. These are a lot less fattening, done with a rub and some olive oil. Double the recipe and refrigerate half for delicious cold snacks.

1. Rinse the wings and set them on paper towels to dry.

2. In a large bowl, mix the rest of the ingredients together. Coat the chicken with the curry mixture, cover, and refrigerate for 1 hour.

3. Grill over medium-hot coals or broil at 350°F for 20 minutes, turning every few minutes, or until well browned.

Serves 4 to 8

4 pounds chicken wings, split at the joint, tips removed
1 tablespoon GF curry powder, or to taste
1 tablespoon onion powder
1 tablespoon garlic powder
¼ teaspoon cinnamon
2 teaspoons dark brown sugar
¼ cup freshly squeezed lime juice
¼ cup olive oil
1 teaspoon salt
Freshly ground black pepper to taste

Grilled Hot-to-Eight-Alarm Chicken Wings

Serves 4 to 8

4 pounds chicken wings, split
    at joint, tips removed
½ pound butter, melted
4–8 teaspoons Tabasco or
    other GF hot pepper sauce
1–2 teaspoons salt, or to taste
Garnish of celery sticks with
    GF blue cheese dressing

The really great part about this recipe is that you can make it as hot as you please. For kids, it's better to use just a bit of heat, not too much.

1. Rinse the chicken and pat dry with paper towels. (If the chicken is wet, the coating won't stick to it.)

2. Mix the butter, Tabasco, and salt in a bowl. Turn the chicken pieces in the bowl to coat.

3. Grill over medium flame or broil at 350°F until chicken is browned and sizzling, about 20 minutes. Be careful not to burn it. Serve with celery and blue cheese dressing.

Stuffed Celery with Gorgonzola and Green Peppercorns

Celery is a great replacement for, not to mention healthier than, crackers when you are on a gluten-free diet.

1. Arrange the celery on a platter, cover, and refrigerate.

2. Mix the rest of the ingredients together. Stuff the celery and serve. You can put this together two or three hours in advance.

3. Garnish with chopped chives, small shrimp, pieces of roasted red pepper, halved black olives, and/or herbs such as parsley, chives, or oregano.

Makes 1½ cups

1 bunch celery, washed and cut into 2-inch lengths
¾ cup GF sour cream
½ cup crumbled Gorgonzola cheese
1 tablespoon lemon juice
1 tablespoon chopped onion
1 teaspoon celery salt
1 teaspoon Tabasco or other GF hot pepper sauce
2 tablespoons green peppercorns, in brine

Baby Back Ribs

Serves 4 to 6

4 pounds baby back ribs, cut
    into 1-rib servings
½ cup vegetable oil
1 cup your favorite GF barbe-
    cue sauce
1 cup GF tomato juice
½ cup orange juice

You can use Asian or any kind of GF barbe-
cue sauce you wish. The trick is to cook the
ribs in the sauce.

1. Fry the ribs in vegetable oil, turning, over
medium-high heat until lightly brown.

2. Add the rest of the ingredients and cover.
Cook over very low heat for 1 hour.

3. Remove the ribs and continue cooking the
sauce until reduced to 1 cup. Serve sauce with
ribs for dipping.

Grilled Cheese on Toasted Cornbread Squares

This recipe is one of the hundreds of goodies you can make if you have Crunchy Cornbread Squares in your fridge or freezer.

1. Arrange the cornbread squares on a baking sheet that you have prepared with GF nonstick spray. Preheat the oven to 350°F.

2. Whirl the rest of the ingredients in the food processor until mixed. Don't worry about making the cheese mixture smooth. Using a teaspoon, place a small mound of cheese/butter mixture on each cornbread square.

3. Bake until the cheese melts, about 10 minutes. You can vary this recipe by adding different herbs, chopped garlic, or any of your favorite flavors.

Stuffings and Spreads

Making spreads and stuffings for any number of things is a great way to use leftovers. You can take a chunk of leftover Brie cheese and put it in the food processor with some chopped onion and a bit of butter or margarine and have a whole new experience. Leftover chicken is excellent for making many different spreads, filling for stuffed celery, or a little sandwich.

Makes 32 small squares

1 recipe Crunchy Cornbread Squares (see page 216)
½ cup soft butter
1 cup cubed Monterey jack cheese
½ cup grated Parmesan cheese
½ cup roasted red peppers, jarred is fine
½ cup chopped sweet red onion

Chickpea Crepes for Stuffing

Makes enough for 8 snacks

1¼ cups cold water
1 egg
1 teaspoon Tabasco or other GF red pepper sauce
1 cup chickpea flour
1 teaspoon salt
1 teaspoon garlic powder (optional)
Vegetable or olive oil for frying

These are so versatile—you can stuff and fold them or roll and stuff them, as you would cannelloni or manicotti, for a meal.

1. Place the water, egg, and Tabasco in a blender or food processor. Whirl, slowly adding the flour. Stop and scrape down the sides.

2. Whirl in the salt and garlic powder. Heat a nonstick pan over medium-high heat and add a teaspoon of olive or vegetable oil.

3. Pour about 2 ounces of batter into the pan, tipping it quickly to spread the batter. Fry for about 3 minutes or until the edges are crisp. Flip carefully, and when golden, place on waxed paper or parchment to cool.

4. Fold or form into tubes. Stuff with fillings from this chapter.

Crepes—A Taste of Elegance

The great thing about all crepes is that they add a touch of elegance and charm to any meal or snack offering. The second great thing is that crepes can be made in advance and then refrigerated or frozen. They are wonderful to have on hand—if unexpected guests show up for cocktails and supper, well, you're all set. The only required pieces of equipment are a blender and a nonstick frying pan.

Hot Hot Dogs

This is a really great way to serve dogs to people on a gluten-free diet. Turning them into a spread is an exciting twist.

1. Prepare a cookie sheet with GF nonstick spray. Preheat the oven to 350°F.

2. Mix the hot dogs, mustard, onion, and relish in a food processor.

3. Spread a teaspoon of the mixture on one quarter of each crepe and fold in half, then in quarters.

4. Bake for about 10 minutes, until hot. Serve with football, soccer, or baseball, and plenty of mustard on the side.

Serves 6 to 8

3 GF hot dogs, grilled, broiled, or boiled
2 teaspoons GF Dijon mustard
2 teaspoons chopped onion
2 teaspoons green or red relish
1 recipe Chickpea Crepes (see page 226)

Curried Chicken

Serves 8

1 recipe Chickpea Crepes (see page 226)
½ pound chicken breast, poached for 10 minutes, or leftover cooked chicken, minced
½ cup plain yogurt
2 teaspoons GF curry powder, or to taste
¼ cup Major Grey's mango chutney

This whole concept is very Middle Eastern. This mixture is to be stuffed in crepes.

1. Stack the crepes with waxed paper between them. Mix together the chicken, curry powder, and chutney. Place a spoonful of the chicken curry mixture on a quarter section of each crepe.

2. Fold in quarters. Place on a platter and serve.

Peanut Butter, Banana, and Bacon Stuffing

This is perfect as an after-school snack for kids on the go. It's also comfort food for grownups.

1. Place the banana and peanut butter next to each other on one end of crepe.

2. Drizzle with honey and sprinkle with crumbled bacon. Fold the peanut butter, honey, and bacon side over the banana and fold again.

Makes 8 to 10 small crepes

1 slice banana per crepe
8 half-teaspoons GF peanut butter
1 recipe Chickpea Crepes (see page 226)
8 half-teaspoons honey
4 slices GF bacon, fried crisp and crumbled

Pepperoni and Cheese Stuffing

Makes 8 to 10 crepes

2 ounces fresh mozzarella
cheese, cut in small pieces
8–10 slices GF pepperoni
1 recipe Chickpea Crepes
(small, about 4 inches
across; see page 226)

This is another tasty idea for stuffing crepes. You can add some roasted red pepper, onion, and a teaspoon of GF canned crushed tomato.

1. Prepare a cookie sheet with GF nonstick spray. Place cheese and pepperoni on a quarter of each crepe. Add anything else you've decided on. If desired, you can place a drop of GF pizza sauce on each crepe just before folding.

2. Bake until cheese melts, about 10 minutes.

Cakes and Goodies

chapter fourteen

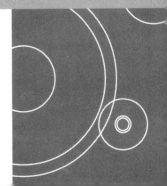

Baked Ricotta Torte with Candied Orange Peel and Chocolate Chips

Serves 6 to 8

5 eggs
1 pound whole-milk ricotta cheese
4 ounces cream cheese (not low- or nonfat)
1 teaspoon vanilla extract
1 teaspoon salt
¾ cup candied orange peel, chopped
1 cup chocolate bits

This is an adaptation of an Italian Christmas torte; it's rich and a very good easy-to-make finale for a big family dinner.

1. Preheat oven to 350°F. Separate the eggs and beat the whites until stiff. Set aside. Put the yolks, cheeses, vanilla, and salt in the food processor and whirl until smooth.

2. Place in a bowl and fold in the egg whites, the orange peel, and the chocolate bits. Prepare a pie plate (preferably glass) with GF nonstick spray. Pour in the egg mixture and bake for 45 minutes or until set and golden on top.

Ricotta Cheese and Cottage Cheese

You can substitute cottage cheese for ricotta in any recipe. Just be sure to use the small-curd, low-salt variety. Cottage cheese may be a bit moister than ricotta—you can drain it by using a sieve and letting the fluid run out, or you can wring it out in cheesecloth.

Chocolate Mint Swirl Cheesecake with Chocolate Nut Crust

This is incredibly rich and delicious. It is definitely a special-occasion cake with layers of deep flavor. Cut the pieces small, as it's very, very rich.

1. Mix the first four ingredients together. Spray a 9-inch springform pan with GF nonstick spray and press the walnut mixture into the bottom to make a crust. Chill for at least 1 hour.

2. Preheat the oven to 350°F. In a clean bowl, beat the egg whites until stiff. Using an electric mixer, beat the cream cheese, sour cream, sugar, vanilla, chestnut flour, and salt in a large bowl. Melt the semisweet chocolate with the schnapps.

3. With the mixer motor running, add the egg yolks to the cream cheese mixture, one at a time, beating vigorously. Fold in the stiff egg whites. Using a knife, swirl the chocolate and schnapps into the bowl.

4. Pour into the springform pan and bake for 1 hour. Turn off the oven, and with the door cracked, let the cake cool for another hour. Chill before serving. You can add whipped cream to the top before serving.

Baking with Cream Cheese

It's best to use cream cheese that is not low- or nonfat. The lower the fat content, the more chemicals there are in the cheese to make it spread easily. When baking, use the purest ingredients, as heat will change the consistency of anything artificial.

Serves 10 to 12

1½ cups ground walnuts (the food processor works well)
½ cup sugar
⅓ cup unsalted butter, melted
4 ounces semisweet chocolate, melted
4 eggs, separated
3 8-ounce packages cream cheese (not low- or nonfat)
1 cup GF sour cream
¾ cup sugar
1½ teaspoons pure vanilla extract
1 teaspoon salt
2 tablespoons chestnut flour
4 ounces semisweet chocolate
2 tablespoons peppermint schnapps
Whipped cream for topping (optional)

Cherry Vanilla Cheesecake with Walnut Crust

Serves 10 to 12

1½ cups ground walnuts
½ cup sugar
½ cup unsalted butter, melted
4 eggs, separated
3 8-ounce packages cream
  cheese
1 cup GF sour cream
2 teaspoons pure vanilla
  extract
1 teaspoon salt
2 tablespoons rice flour
⅔ cup cherry preserves,
  melted

This is a fine combination, with a delightful flavor and smooth consistency.

1. Mix together the walnuts, sugar, and melted butter. Prepare a 9-inch springform pan with GF nonstick spray and press the nut mixture into the bottom to form a crust. Chill for at least 1 hour.

2. Preheat oven to 350°F. Beat the egg whites and set aside. In a large bowl, using an electric mixer, beat the cream cheese, sour cream, vanilla, salt, and rice flour together.

3. Add the egg yolks, one at a time, while beating. When smooth, fold in the egg whites and mix in the cherry preserves.

4. Pour into springform pan and bake for 1 hour. Turn off oven and crack the door. Let cake cool for another hour. Chill before serving.

Nut Crusts for Cheesecake

We specify walnuts because they are probably the least expensive shelled nut and work well in these recipes. However, you can substitute hazelnuts, almonds, or pecans. Pecans add a Southern touch and are really good—and expensive. Grinding nuts is simple—just use your food processor.

Lemon Cheesecake with Nut Crust

This cheesecake is light, with an intense lemon flavor. It's a good summer cheesecake that will make your guests ask for more.

1. Mix together the ground nuts, sugar, and melted butter. Use GF nonstick spray on a 9-inch springform pan. Press the nut mixture into the bottom to form a crust, and chill.

2. Preheat oven to 350°F. Beat the egg whites until stiff and set aside. Using an electric mixer, beat the cheese, sour cream, sugar, flour, salt, and egg yolks, adding the yolks one at a time. Beat in the lemon juice and lemon rind.

3. Gently fold in the egg whites. Pour the cheese/lemon mixture into the springform. Bake for 1 hour. Turn off oven and crack the door, letting cool for another hour. Chill before serving. The chopped nuts and thinly sliced lemon make a nice touch.

Stiffly Beaten Egg Whites

Be very careful not to get even a speck of egg yolk in the whites to be beaten stiff. Even a drop of egg yolk will prevent the whites from stiffening. And always use clean beaters. Any fat or oil will prevent the whites from fluffing up. You can use a drop of vinegar or lemon juice to help them stiffen up.

Serves 10 to 12

1¼ cups ground walnuts (or whatever nuts you like)
½ cup sugar
½ cup unsalted butter, melted
5 egg whites
3 8-ounce packages cream cheese
1 cup GF sour cream
⅔ cup sugar
2 tablespoons rice flour
3 egg yolks
Juice of one lemon
Minced rind of 1 lemon
1 teaspoon salt
Extra nuts to sprinkle on top of cake
Paper-thin lemon slices

Molten Lava
Dark Chocolate Cake

Serves 8

8 teaspoons butter to grease custard cups

8 tablespoons sugar to coat buttered custard cups

8 ounces semisweet baking chocolate

6 ounces unsalted butter

3 eggs

3 egg yolks

⅓ cup sugar

1 tablespoon chestnut flour

1 teaspoon vanilla

1 quart raspberry sorbet

For such an easy recipe, it comes off as elegant. It just tastes more complex than it is to make. The nice thing is that the chestnut flour gives a wonderful underlying flavor.

1. Prepare the insides of eight 6-ounce custard cups with butter and sugar. Preheat oven to 425°F. Over very low heat, melt the chocolate and butter in a heavy saucepan.

2. Beat the eggs, egg yolks, sugar, flour, and vanilla for about 10 minutes. Add the chocolate mixture by the tablespoonful until the eggs have digested some of the chocolate. Fold in the rest of the chocolate/butter mixture.

3. Divide the mixture between the custard cups. Place the cups on a cookie sheet and bake for 12 to 13 minutes. The sides should be puffed and the center very soft. Serve hot with raspberry sorbet spooned into the "craters."

Raspberry Coulis

You can use any berry. Heavily seeded berries can be strained though a fine sieve or cheesecloth. Various liqueurs also make nice additions.

Place berries in a saucepan with the sugar and water, juice, or liqueur. Bring to a boil. Cool and strain.

Makes 1½ cups

1 pint raspberries
½ cup sugar
¼ cup water, orange juice, or fruit liqueur such as peach or cherry

Strawberry-Blueberry Coulis

Makes 1½ cups

½ pint blueberries, rinsed
½ pint strawberries, rinsed
¼ cup water
¼ cup sugar
1" by ½" strip orange rind

This is wonderful not only on crepes but on GF ice cream and pancakes as well.

Place all of the ingredients in a saucepan and bring to a boil. Remove from the heat and cool. Whisk until smooth. Serve warm or cool.

Molten Sweet
White Chocolate Cake

This is delicious with fresh berries and whipped cream spooned into the "craters."

1. Prepare the insides of eight 6-ounce custard cups with butter and sugar. Preheat oven to 425°F. Melt the chocolate and butter over low heat in a heavy saucepan. In a large bowl, using an electric mixer, beat together the eggs, egg yolks, sugar, and flour. Add vanilla and salt.

2. Keep beating and slowly add, by the tablespoonful, one-fourth of the white chocolate mixture. When well blended, very slowly add the rest of the chocolate mixture.

3. Divide between the custard cups, place on a cookie sheet, and bake for about 12 minutes. Serve with mixed berries in the "craters." You can also vary this by using shaved bittersweet chocolate in the craters, or you can spoon in GF ice cream or sorbet.

Serves 8

8 teaspoons butter to grease custard cups
8 tablespoons sugar to coat buttered custard cups
8 ounces unsweetened white baking chocolate
6 ounces unsalted butter
3 eggs
3 egg yolks
⅓ cup sugar
1 tablespoon chestnut flour
1 teaspoon vanilla
½ teaspoon salt
2 cups mixed berries, such as strawberries, raspberries, and blueberries

Orange Carrot Cake

Serves 8 to 10

4 eggs, separated
½ cup brown sugar
1½ cups grated carrots
1 tablespoon lemon juice
Grated rind of ½ fresh orange
½ cup corn flour
1 inch fresh ginger root,
    peeled and minced
1½ teaspoons baking soda
½ teaspoon salt

This delicious cake has a nice zing with the addition of a little lemon juice and the grated orange rind. The ginger root adds an appealing sophistication.

1. Liberally butter a 9-inch springform pan and preheat oven to 325°F. Beat the egg whites until stiff and set aside.

2. Beat the egg yolks, sugar, and carrots together. Add lemon juice, orange rind, and corn flour. When smooth, add the gingerroot, baking soda, and salt. Gently fold in the egg whites.

3. Pour the cake batter into the springform pan and bake for 1 hour. Test by plunging a toothpick into the center of the cake—if the pick comes out clean, the cake is done.

What's Up, Doc?

Carrot cake was created during World War II when flour and sugar were rationed. The sweetness of carrots contributed to this cake, and when oranges were available, it became a feast. Cooks used their fuel carefully too, baking and making stews and soups in the oven all at the same time. Sometimes, hard times make for sweet endings.

Classic Pavlova Cake

This light, beautiful, delicate, and delicious cake is enhanced by sweet bananas and strawberries.

1. Preheat oven to 200°F.

2. Whip the egg whites, and as they stiffen, add the vinegar and slowly add the sugar. Pour into a 9-inch glass pie pan that you've treated with GF nonstick spray.

3. Bake the meringue for 2 hours. Then, turn off the oven and crack the door. Let the meringue rest for another hour. It should become very crisp and lightly browned. Do not store it if the weather is humid.

4. Whip the cream and mix in the confectioners' sugar and vanilla. Slice a layer of bananas onto the bottom of the cooled meringue crust. Add a layer of whipped cream. Sprinkle with halved strawberries.

5. Add another layer of whipped cream and decorate with the whole strawberries. Serve immediately or it will get soggy.

Origins of the Pavlova

There is some discussion as to who invented this cake. It was designed to honor the famed ballerina Anna Pavlova, whose admirers came from around the world. Some say it was created in Australia; others say the cake was born in the United States.

Serves 6

4 egg whites
1 teaspoon vinegar
4 ounces sugar
1 cup heavy cream
3 tablespoons confectioners' sugar
½ teaspoon vanilla
1 banana, sliced
1 quart strawberries, washed, hulled, and halved, 8 left whole for decoration

Pavlova with Chocolate and Bananas

Serves 6

4 egg whites
1 teaspoon vinegar
4 ounces sugar
3 squares semisweet chocolate
½ cup unsalted butter
⅓ cup sugar
2 bananas, kept in the freezer for 20 minutes to firm
1 cup heavy cream, whipped with 2 teaspoons confectioners' sugar

The uses of meringue are myriad—we are giving you just a few.

1. Preheat oven to 200°F.

2. Whip the egg whites, and as they stiffen, add the vinegar and slowly add the sugar. Pour into a 9-inch glass pie pan that you've treated with GF nonstick spray.

3. Bake the meringue for 2 hours. Then, turn off the oven and crack the door. Let the meringue rest for another hour. It should become very crisp and lightly browned. Do not store it if the weather is humid.

4. Melt the chocolate, butter, and sugar. Cool until it's still liquid but room temperature.

5. Peel and slice 1 banana into the meringue crust. Spoon half of the GF chocolate sauce over it. Add the other banana and the remaining sauce, and top with whipped cream.

Blanching

When you blanch a peach, a tomato, or a nectarine, you plunge it into boiling water for a minute. You don't cook it, you just loosen the skin. If you are blanching a great many pieces, have a colander next to your pot of boiling water and a pot of ice water in the sink. Use a slotted spoon to remove the fruit from the boiling water, put it into the colander, and then plunge it into the ice water. After it is cool enough to handle, slip off the skin and cut it up.

Pavlova with Peach Melba Cream

If you love peach melba, you'll absolutely flip over this dessert. With the crisp meringue, it's just as good as it gets.

1. Preheat oven to 200°F.

2. Whip the egg whites, and as they stiffen, add the vinegar and slowly add the sugar. Pour into a 9-inch glass pie pan that you've treated with GF nonstick spray.

3. Bake the meringue for 2 hours. Then, turn off the oven and crack the door open. Let the meringue rest for another hour. It should become very crisp and lightly browned. Do not store it if the weather is humid.

4. Place the water and gelatin in the blender. Bring a saucepan of water to a boil. Add the peaches, and when the skin is loosened, remove the peaches and cool.

5. Slip off the peach skin. Pit the peaches and chop them. Add the peaches to the gelatin and water in your blender. Blend, and then let cool to room temperature.

6. Just before serving, fold the beaten egg whites into the peach mixture. Fold in the whipped cream. Fill the meringue shell with the peach mixture and sprinkle with raspberries.

Serves 6

4 egg whites
1 teaspoon vinegar
4 ounces sugar
4 ounces cool water
1 (¼-ounce) package unfla-vored gelatin
4 peaches
3 egg whites, beaten stiff
1 cup heavy cream, beaten stiff
½ pint fresh raspberries, rinsed and dried on paper towels

Meringue Cups with Icy Sorbet and Fruit Filling

Serves 4

6 egg whites
1 teaspoon vinegar
5 ounces sugar
½ cup walnut pieces, coarsely chopped
4 scoops raspberry or strawberry sorbet
Garnish of 4 teaspoons chocolate bits or shaved semisweet chocolate
1 cup heavy cream, whipped with 2 tablespoons sugar

Follow your taste preferences when filling these meringues—try different flavors of sorbet and fruit.

1. Beat the egg whites, slowly adding the vinegar and sugar. Fold in the nuts. Preheat the oven to 250°F.

2. Prepare four 6-ounce custard cups with GF nonstick spray. Spoon the egg-white mixture into the cups, using a spoon to make a depression in the center of each.

3. Bake for 1 hour. Then turn off oven and crack the door open and check to make sure the cups are cooked through and crisp.

4. Fill the cups with fruit sorbet or GF ice cream. Top with chocolate bits, or shaved chocolate and whipped cream.

Meringues Are Perfect for Gluten-Free Desserts

Meringues are low-calorie, being made of egg white, and you can substitute artificial sweetener for sugar and eat the sweets to your heart's content. Meringue can be flavored with chocolate, vanilla, and fruit liqueurs. Meringue cups can be filled with anything you like, from ices to GF ice cream.

Chestnut Cookies

These are festive and delicious. Make a lot for a party or to give to friends.

1. Drain the chestnuts and chop in the food processor. Place in the bowl of an electric mixer. With the motor on low, add the chestnut flour, milk, egg yolks, vanilla, salt, baking powder, sugar, and melted butter.

2. Preheat the oven to 350°F. Fold the egg whites into the chestnut mixture. Drop by the teaspoonful on cookie sheets lined with parchment paper.

3. Bake for 12 to 15 minutes. Cool and place on platters for immediate use, or store in tins for later use.

Chestnuts—Raw, Jarred, or Canned?

Preparing chestnuts can be a real pain! You have to make cross slits in each, then either boil or roast them, and get the shells off. Then, you have to peel off the skins. This process is time consuming. However, you can buy pre-pared chestnuts in jars and cans and avoid all that work. Of course, your house won't smell like roasted chestnuts, but you'll have more time to enjoy them.

Make about 48 cookies

1 2-ounce can chestnuts, roasted, peeled, and packed in water
1½ cups chestnut flour
½ cup milk
2 egg yolks
1 teaspoon vanilla
1 teaspoon salt
2 teaspoons GF baking powder
½ cup granulated sugar
½ cup unsalted butter, melted
3 egg whites, beaten stiff

Chocolate Meringue and Nut Cookies

Makes about 40 cookies

½ cup sugar, divided
¼ cup unsweetened cocoa powder
⅛ teaspoon salt
3 egg whites (from extra-large eggs)
⅛ teaspoon cream of tartar
½ cup hazelnuts, lightly toasted, skinned, and coarsely chopped

These are crisp and delicious. The nuts add a wonderful crunch. Use either blanched almonds or hazelnuts.

1. Preheat oven to 275°F. Line two cookie sheets with parchment paper. Sift ¼ cup of sugar and ¼ cup of cocoa together in a bowl. Add salt.

2. Beat egg whites with cream of tartar. When peaks begin to form, add the remaining ¼ cup sugar, a teaspoon at a time. Slowly beat in the cocoa mixture. The meringue should be stiff and shiny.

3. Add chopped nuts. Drop by teaspoonfuls on the parchment paper. Bake for 45 to 50 minutes. Cool on baking sheets. You can store these in an airtight cookie tin or serve them the same day.

Ugly, but Good!

These cookies are known in Italy as "ugly but good"! Other, kinder descriptions include "kisses" and "crisps." They are a bit dumpy looking, but just try one. This recipe is a simplification of the original, far more time-consuming one.

Apple Cobbler with Cheddar Biscuit Crust

This cobbler is very easy to make in advance—
just give yourself an hour to bake it before
serving.

1. Preheat the oven to 325°F. In a large bowl,
mix the flour, salt, baking powder, and pepper.
Cut in the margarine with a large fork until it
looks like oatmeal. Add the buttermilk and stir.
Add the cheese and set aside.

2. Place the apples in a large baking dish,
about 9" x 13", or a 2-quart casserole. Sprinkle
them with lemon juice.

3. Mix together the spices, cornstarch, sugars,
and salt. Toss the apples with this mixture. Dot
with butter. Drop the cheese mixture by the
tablespoonful over the top.

4. Bake for 50 minutes, or until crust is
browned and the apples are bubbling. Serve
with extra slices of cheese or with GF vanilla
ice cream.

Serves 8 to 10

2 cups corn flour
½ teaspoon salt
4 teaspoons GF baking powder
½ teaspoon cayenne pepper
¼ cup margarine, softened
¾ cup buttermilk
¾ cup grated sharp Cheddar
    cheese
8 large tart apples such as
    Granny Smiths, peeled,
    cored, and sliced
⅓ cup lemon juice
2 teaspoons cinnamon
¼ teaspoon nutmeg
1½ tablespoons cornstarch
¼ cup dark brown sugar
¼ cup white sugar
Pinch salt
4 tablespoons butter

Blueberry-Peach Cobbler

Serves 10

6 ripe peaches, blanched in boiling water, skinned, pitted, and sliced
½ cup fresh lemon juice
1 cup sugar, divided
1 pint blueberries, rinsed and picked over, stems removed
1 stick (½ cup) unsalted butter, melted
½ teaspoon salt
1½ cups rice flour or quinoa flour
1 tablespoon GF baking powder
1 cup buttermilk

This smells and tastes like August; however, if you blanch and freeze your peaches and buy frozen blueberries, you can reminisce over a past August in January.

1. Preheat the oven to 375°F. Slice peaches into a bowl and sprinkle with lemon juice and ½ cup sugar. Add the blueberries and mix well.

2. Prepare a 9" x 13" baking dish with GF nonstick spray. Spread the peaches and blueberries on the bottom. Pour the melted butter into a large bowl. Add the remaining ½ cup sugar and salt and whisk in the flour and baking powder. Add the buttermilk and stir; don't worry about lumps.

3. Drop the batter by tablespoonfuls over the fruit. Bake for 35 to 40 minutes. Cool for 25 minutes. Serve with GF vanilla ice cream or whipped cream.

Orange Cornmeal Cookies

This is an adaptation of a classic Italian cookie. You will love them for the kids and can add currants, raisins, or dried apple chips.

1. Whirl the eggs and sugar in the bowl of your food processor. Slowly add the rest of the ingredients, stopping occasionally to scrape the bowl.

2. Don't overprocess. When the dough comes together, remove from the food processor and place in plastic wrap. Refrigerate for 1 to 2 hours.

3. Preheat oven to 350°F. Prepare a cookie sheet with GF nonstick spray or parchment paper.

4. Shape the dough into a flat oval. Break off a small piece and roll into a ball. Flatten and place on cookie sheet. Repeat until all of the dough is used. Bake for 10 minutes, or until golden.

Makes 30 cookies

3 eggs
1 cup sugar
1½ cups cornmeal (yellow)
1¼ cup corn flour
½ teaspoon salt
¾ teaspoon xanthan gum
1½ sticks (¾ cup) unsalted butter, melted
1 tablespoon concentrated orange juice
Zest of ½ orange, very finely minced

Puddings, Mousses and Souffles

chapter fifteen

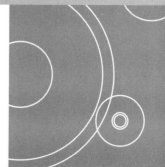

Apple Brown Betty with Cornbread

Serves 4

4 large tart apples, peeled, cored, and sliced
Juice of ½ lemon
2 cups cornbread cubes
2 eggs, lightly beaten
1½ cups milk
1 teaspoon vanilla extract
¼ teaspoon ground nutmeg
1 teaspoon ground cinnamon
⅛ teaspoon ground cloves
½ teaspoon salt
½ cup dark brown sugar, or to taste
½ cup butter

In the early days of the United States, no food went to waste. Thus, stale bread was made into a delicious, homey baked pudding.

1. Preheat oven to 350°F. Liberally butter a 2-quart casserole dish or treat it with nonstick spray.

2. Put the apples in the casserole and sprinkle with lemon juice. Add the bread cubes. Mix well.

3. Beat together the eggs, milk, vanilla, spices, salt, and sugar. Mix with the apples and bread cubes. Dot with butter.

4. Bake for 45 minutes, or until brown on top and very moist inside. Serve warm with whipped cream or ice cream.

Why Not Use Canned Whipped Cream?

Whipped cream that comes in aerosol spray cans is much sweeter than the cream you would whip yourself. Also, there is more air than cream, so you are paying a premium for the spray convenience. When you do your own cream whipping, you will get a lot more flavor, no additives, and a healthier end product.

Indian Pudding with Whipped Cream

If you make too much, let it firm up and fry it in butter, making sweet griddle cakes for breakfast the next day.

1. Preheat the oven to 250°F. Heat 2 cups milk. Place the cornmeal and the rest of the dry ingredients, the gingerroot, and molasses in the top of a double boiler.

2. Whisk the hot milk into the mixture, cooking and stirring over simmering water for 10 minutes or until smooth. Prepare a casserole dish with butter or nonstick spray.

3. Whisk the cold milk into the hot mixture and pour into the baking dish. Bake for 3 hours. Serve hot or at room temperature with whipped cream.

Serves 8

4 cups milk, divided
¼ cup white or yellow cornmeal
⅓ cup dark brown sugar
¼ cup white sugar
1 teaspoon salt
1 teaspoon cinnamon
¼ teaspoon ground nutmeg
1 teaspoon minced fresh gingerroot
¼ cup molasses
5 tablespoons unsalted butter

Swedish Fruit Pudding (Kram)

Serves 4

1 10-ounce box frozen strawberries
1 10-ounce box frozen raspberries
¼ cup lemon juice
1½ tablespoons arrowroot
flour or cornstarch
Pinch salt
¼ cup sugar, or to taste
2 tablespoons orange liqueur
(optional)
GF whipped cream or ice
cream

Children and adults like this equally well.
It's tangy and very bright red. Serve it in
wineglasses with a spoonful of whipped
cream on top.

1. Place the thawed berries in a saucepan.
Drain off the juice that is produced from thaw-
ing into a bowl. Mix in the lemon juice. Add the
arrowroot or cornstarch to the mixture.

2. Stir the liquid and a pinch of salt into the
berries. Cook over low heat until the mixture
starts to thicken. Add the liqueur. Cool and
serve in wineglasses with whipped cream.

Kram with Lingonber-
ries or Cloudberries

A variation on the traditional Scandinavian
pudding, with the sweetness of summer berries.

1. Place the berries and sugar in a saucepan.

2. Mix the cornstarch with cold water in a separate cup until smooth. Add to the berries.

3. Simmer over low heat until the mixture
thickens. Cool. Whip the cream and add to the
berry mixture.

Serves 4

14 ounces lingonberries
   or cloudberries, fresh or
   frozen, thawed
½ cup sugar or to taste
3 tablespoons cornstarch or
   arrowroot flour
½ cup cold water
1 cup heavy cream whipped
   with 1 teaspoon sugar

Plum Parfait

Serves 4

1½ teaspoons unflavored
    gelatin
2 tablespoons water
½ cup sugar, or to taste
4 purple or red plums
1 cup water
1-inch strip orange rind
1 cup heavy cream, whipped
    with 1 tablespoon sugar

This is really easy, and pretty. But you must have fresh, large, sweet plums. Skip it if the plums are wizened or small.

1. In the jar of the blender, sprinkle the gelatin over the cold water. Let sit until the gelatin "blooms."

2. In a saucepan, mix the sugar, plums, orange rind, and water; bring to a boil. Pour the sugar/water over the gelatin and blend. When the plums are cool enough to handle, remove the pits and add the fruit to the blender, skin and all.

3. Spoon cooled plum mixture into wineglasses, making layers with the whipped cream. Swirl with a knife. Chill and serve.

Panna Cotta

This classic Italian dessert has multiple variations—you can make it with cream, milk, yogurt, or buttermilk, or a mixture of these four.

1. Mix the water and gelatin together and let rest until gelatin "blooms," about 5 minutes.

2. Stir the cream and sugar in a saucepan over moderate heat until sugar dissolves. Do not boil. Whisk in the gelatin and water; cool to room temperature. Whisk in buttermilk and vanilla.

3. Prepare six 6-ounce custard cups with nonstick spray. Divide the custard between the cups. Refrigerate for 6 hours or overnight.

4. Run a sharp knife around the edge of each cup. Invert the cups on chilled plates. Serve with fruit coulis, fresh berries, or both.

Panna Cotta Flan Custard

Panna cotta, the Italian custard dessert, is basically a custard made with buttermilk. Flan is also a custard and may be made with fruit. Custard is made with eggs, milk, sugar, and flavoring. Simple and easy to digest, these custards are basics for adults and children.

Serves 6

2 teaspoons water
2 teaspoons unflavored gelatin
1 cup whipping cream
⅓ cup sugar, or to taste
2 cups lowfat buttermilk, well shaken
1 teaspoon vanilla
Fruit coulis or fresh fruit of your choice

Strawberry Clouds

Serves 4

1 (¼-ounce) package unflavored gelatin
¼ cup cold water
1 cup boiling water
1 pint strawberries, rinsed and
   hulled
Sugar to taste
2 egg whites, beaten stiff
½ cup heavy cream, beaten
   stiff with 1 tablespoon
   sugar

These fluffy delights are cool and refreshing. Garnish with sprigs of mint. The recipe
is a cross between a Bavarian cream and a
mousse.

1. Place the gelatin and water in the bowl of
your blender. Let stand for 5 minutes so the
gelatin can "bloom." With the motor running,
slowly pour in the boiling water.

2. Add strawberries and sugar. Whirl until
smooth, stopping to scrape down the sides of
the jar.

3. When the berries have cooled, fold in the
egg whites and whipped cream. Refrigerate
until chilled, mixing occasionally.

Clouds

You can use berries as a flavoring for clouds,
but peaches, blanched and mashed, are also
very good, as are pears. Try making a cloud
with fresh, spicy applesauce for fall. The basic
principle works with all fruits. Just vary the
amount of sugar to suit the type of fruit; that is,
if the fruit is very sweet, use less sugar.

Lemon Clouds

Cool and delicious—this is a delight, any time of year.

1. In the jar of the blender, sprinkle the gelatin over the water. Let rest for 4 to 5 minutes. Add the lemon juice, lemon rind, sugar, boiling water, and butter. Blend until well mixed. Cool.

2. Beat the egg whites until stiff. Fold them into the lemon mixture. Chill in the refrigerator, stirring every half hour. Place in individual glasses or bowls. Serve with lots of fresh berries.

Serves 4 to 6

1½ teaspoons unflavored gelatin
2 tablespoons cool water
Juice of 1 fresh lemon
1 tablespoon minced lemon rind
½ cup sugar, or to taste
1 cup boiling water
2 tablespoons unsalted butter
4 egg whites

Hot Butter Pecan Sauce

Makes 1 cup

½ cup dark brown sugar
½ cup white sugar
Pinch salt
1 teaspoon vanilla
¼ cup heavy cream
1 cup pecan pieces

This couldn't be richer or lovelier over ice cream, sorbet, or crepes. Nuts add a wonderful crunch.

1. Combine sugars and salt in a heavy-bottomed saucepan. Heat, stirring, until sugars melt; bring to a boil.

2. Cook over high heat until caramelized. Remove from heat and add vanilla and cream. Add nuts, stir, and serve hot.

Chocolate Mousse

The classic darling of the French bistro, this is a fresh take on an old favorite.

1. Combine the chocolate, rum or cognac, and sugar in a heavy saucepan or the top of a double boiler. Mix the coffee powder with boiling water and add to the chocolate mixture.

2. Cook over very low heat, stirring from time to time, until the chocolate melts. Remove from the heat and cool for 3 minutes. Slowly beat in the egg yolks, one at a time.

3. Let cool and fold in the egg whites. Spoon into a serving bowl or dessert glasses. Chill for 4 to 6 hours. Serve with whipped cream.

Garnishes for Chocolate Mousse

Fresh raspberries are perfect garnishes for chocolate mousse, as are sprigs of mint. You can also pour a bit of peppermint schnapps over each serving for an added kick. Chambord, raspberry liqueur, is also good added to the mousse when you are making it.

Serves 6 to 8

4 squares semisweet chocolate
¼ cup rum or cognac
½ cup sugar, or to taste
1 teaspoon instant coffee powder
¼ cup boiling water
5 eggs, separated
1 cup heavy cream, whipped stiff with 1 tablespoon sugar

Chocolate-Raspberry Soufflé

Serves 4

2 squares bittersweet
   chocolate
½ cup sugar
1 tablespoon butter plus 1
   tablespoon for soufflé dish
2 tablespoons Chambord
   (raspberry liqueur)
3 tablespoons rice flour or
   cornstarch
3 tablespoons cold milk
4 egg yolks
5 egg whites
Pinch cream of tartar
½ pint fresh raspberries,
   rinsed and allowed to dry
   on paper towels

Chocolate and raspberries are a heavenly combination. Serving a soufflé is grand enough, but adding fresh raspberries to the mix is very special.

1. Preheat the oven to 375°F.

2. In a medium-sized, heavy saucepan, melt the chocolate with the sugar, butter, and Chambord. Remove from heat. Whisk the flour and milk together and add to the chocolate mixture.

3. Beat the egg yolks, one at a time, into the chocolate mixture. Whip the egg whites and cream of tartar together until stiff. Fold the egg whites into the chocolate mixture and pour into a buttered 1½-quart soufflé dish.

4. Bake for 35 to 40 minutes or until puffed and brown. Pour fresh raspberries over each portion and garnish with whipped cream if desired.

The Creative Soufflé

The variety of soufflés you can make is limited only by the availability of ingredients and your imagination. You can substitute mashed bananas for the chocolate, or mangos, for that matter. The soufflé makes a marvelous presentation, but it must be served immediately or it will flop.

Espresso Custard

This silky, rich custard can be served with whipped cream or coffee ice cream.

1. Preheat oven to 325°F. Whisk together the espresso powder and boiling water, add the cream, and beat in the eggs. Whisk the cornstarch and water together until smooth and beat into the mixture.

2. Add the rest of the ingredients and stir well. Place four buttered 6-ounce custard cups in a roasting pan of hot water in the middle of the oven. Add the custard.

3. Bake for 50 to 60 minutes. Serve warm, room temperature, or chilled with whipped cream.

Espresso

Espresso coffee beans are roasted longer than the beans for regular coffee; that's why they have such a dark and deep flavor. In cooking, use instant espresso powder, and you certainly can use decaf espresso powder for equally good results, with no caffeine buzz.

Serves 4

3 tablespoons instant espresso powder
2 tablespoons boiling water
2 cups whipping cream
3 whole eggs
4 teaspoons cornstarch
4 teaspoons cold water
½ cup sugar, or to taste
1 teaspoon vanilla

Half-Frozen Mocha Mousse

Serves 4

2 tablespoons espresso
    powder
4 tablespoons pure, Dutch
    cocoa powder
⅓ cup ice water
⅔ cup sugar
1 teaspoon vanilla
½ teaspoon salt
1 cup heavy cream

Mocha, the combination of coffee and chocolate, is said to be an aphrodisiac. And when
it's frozen enough to be icy cold and very
dark, it could evoke Eros.

1. Blend the espresso powder, cocoa powder,
and water together until smooth. Add sugar,
vanilla, and salt.

2. Whip the cream and fold the cocoa mixture
into it, mixing gently but thoroughly.

3. Place in a bowl in the freezer for 1 hour, stirring occasionally; do not freeze hard. Serve
in balloon wineglasses with shaved chocolate
sprinkled over the top.

Pumpkin Custard

You can substitute frozen winter (butternut) squash for the pumpkin with good results. Canned pumpkin is very heavy and strong, so try to avoid it.

1. Preheat oven to 325°F. Puree the pumpkin in your blender or food processor. Slowly add the rest of the ingredients.

2. Pour into a buttered casserole dish. Place a roasting pan of hot water in the middle of the oven. Put the bowl of pumpkin custard in the roasting pan and bake for 50 to 60 minutes. A nice variation is to add a cup of pecan pieces and let them bake right in the custard.

Serves 6 to 8

2 cups cubed fresh pumpkin, steamed in 1 cup water, or 2 (12–13 ounce) packages frozen winter squash, thawed
½ cup brown sugar
¼ cup white sugar
½ teaspoon each: ground ginger, ground cloves, ground nutmeg
1 teaspoon ground cinnamon
3 eggs, beaten
1 cup heavy cream

Rice Pudding with Apricots

Serves 6 to 8

1 cup dried apricots, cut into
   quarters
1 cup water
½ cup sugar
1 cup rice (basmati is prefer-
   able)
2½ cups milk
1 teaspoon vanilla
⅛ teaspoon nutmeg
½ cup sugar, more to taste
1 cup heavy cream, whipped
   stiff
8 ounces blanched almonds,
   toasted, for garnish

The classic recipe mixes canned cherries in heavy syrup with the rice pudding. This is a bit different and, we think, better.

1. Bring the apricots, water, and sugar to a boil and turn down heat. Simmer until the apricots are plump and the sauce syrupy.

2. In a large, heavy pot, mix the rice and milk. Bring to a boil and then turn down heat to simmer and cook for about 60 minutes, stirring occasionally.

3. Add the vanilla, nutmeg, and sugar, stirring. Cool slightly. Whip the cream and fold it into the pudding. Fold the apricots into the pudding. Top with toasted almonds.

Chocolate Sauce

An essential topping for ice cream, rice pudding, and other desserts. This sauce will keep, refrigerated, for 2 weeks or longer.

Combine all ingredients in a heavy saucepan. Cook, stirring, until sauce is thickened and the sugar is dissolved. Store in a jar in the refrigerator.

Makes 1 cup

2 ounces semisweet chocolate
½ cup water
½ cup sugar, or to taste
1 teaspoon vanilla extract
2 tablespoons unsalted butter
¼ teaspoon salt

Fried Polenta Squares with Salsa

Guacamole

Gravlax (Salmon Cured in Sugar and Salt)

Cucumber Sauce for Gravlax

Mustard Sauce for Gravlax, Ham, or Roast Beef

Hot or Cold Asparagus Soup

Tiny Garbanzo Crepes

Cheese Fondue with Dipping Vegetables

Grilled Eggplant and Pepper Salad

Paella

Stuffed, Roasted Filet Mignon

Chocolate-Dipped Strawberries

Dark Chocolate, Walnut, and Hazelnut Torte

Recipes for
a Dinner Party

chapter sixteen

Fried Polenta Squares with Salsa

Makes 12 to 24 squares

6½ cups of water
2 tablespoons salt
2 cups yellow cornmeal
2–4 ounces unsalted butter
2 tablespoons dried herbs or 1
tablespoon each fresh basil,
rosemary, and parsley
½ cup freshly grated Parmesan cheese
Freshly ground black pepper
to taste
2 tablespoons unsalted butter
and 2–4 tablespoons
vegetable oil, for frying
1 8-ounce jar of your favorite
salsa or homemade
Guacamole (see page 271)
for dipping

Make the polenta a day in advance, then refrigerate it until just before the party.

1. Bring the water to a boil.

2. Add salt, and using your hand, drop the cornmeal into the boiling water, letting it slip slowly between your fingers to make a very slim stream. You should be able to see each grain. Do not dump the cornmeal into the water or you will get a mass of glue.

3. Stir constantly while adding the cornmeal. Reduce heat to a simmer and keep stirring for about 20 minutes as it thickens.

4. Stir in the butter, herbs, Parmesan cheese, and pepper. Spread in a 9" x 13" glass pan that has been prepared with nonstick spray.

5. Chill for 3 hours or overnight. Cut into squares and fry until golden brown over medium heat in a combination of butter and oil. If you are having an outdoor party, you can grill the squares over low flame for a smoky flavor. Serve with salsa or guacamole.

Guacamole

There are many recipes for guacamole. Some employ adobo sauce, others use tomatoes, and still others combine lemon and lime juice.

Using a fork, mash the avocados, mixing in the rest of the ingredients until well blended.

Choosing Avocados

Most store-bought avocados are as hard as stones. That's fine; if you buy ripe ones, they generally have many blemishes. Just buy them a few days before you plan to serve them. Place them on a sunny window sill or in a brown paper bag or wrap them in a newspaper. The paper seems to hasten ripening. The avocado should not have oily black spots in it when you cut it open but should be a uniform green. One or two black spots can be cut out, but don't use an avocado that is full of black spots or gray-brown areas.

Makes 1 to 1½ cups

3 medium Hass avocados or 2 large, smooth-skinned ones, peeled and seeded

Juice of 2 limes

½ cup finely minced sweet onion

1 teaspoon Tabasco sauce, or to taste

½ teaspoon salt, or to taste

2 tablespoons finely chopped fresh cilantro

Gravlax (Salmon Cured in Sugar and Salt)

Serves 12 to 15

1 3-pound salmon filet, skin removed
⅔ cup salt
½ cup granulated sugar
20 white peppercorns, crushed
6 thick slices fresh ginger root, peeled
5 large fronds fresh dill weed
1 recipe Cucumber Sauce (see page 273)
1 recipe Mustard Sauce (see page 274)

This is a year-round Swedish specialty—good on any buffet at any special occasion. The salmon will "cook" or "cure" in the salt and sugar.

1. Rinse the salmon and dry on paper towels.

2. In a large glass baking pan, mix together the salt, sugar, and pepper. Place the salmon in the pan and turn it to cover with the mixture.

3. Arrange the ginger root over and under the fish. Place fronds of dill over and under the fish. Cover tightly and refrigerate for 16 to 24 hours.

4. Scrape off the salt and sugar, wiping the fish with paper towels. Slice thinly, on the diagonal, and serve with sprigs of watercress, hard-boiled egg slices, and the dressings.

Cucumber Sauce for Gravlax

This is such a great side with Gravlax. It's also good with cold roast beef or roasted filet mignon or ham.

1. Slice the cucumber in half lengthwise and scoop out the seeds and discard. Chop the cucumber finely.

2. Add the rest of the ingredients, except the chives and parsley, and store in the refrigerator for at least 2 hours to "marry," which will bring out the flavors.

3. Serve in a chilled bowl alongside the gravlax. Garnish with chives and parsley.

Makes 3 cups

1 long English cucumber (also known as Burpee's Burpless), peeled
1 red onion, chopped fine
1½ cups sour cream
½ cup minced fresh dill
Juice and minced zest of 1 lemon
1 teaspoon champagne vinegar or other white wine vinegar
1 teaspoon salt
Black or white pepper, freshly ground, to taste
Chopped chives and parsley for garnish

Mustard Sauce for Gravlax, Ham, or Roast Beef

Makes 1 cup

⅔ cup olive oil
⅓ cup white wine vinegar
1 tablespoon Dijon-style mustard
1 teaspoon sugar
Salt and pepper to taste
Fresh herbs such as dill, oregano, parsley, or basil

This is so simple and good, you won't ever go wrong by making it. You can also serve it with salads.

Place all ingredients in a blender and whirl until emulsified. Serve in a glass bowl or sauceboat. Store in a glass jar, covered, in the refrigerator. Will keep for a week, depending on the freshness of the herbs. It will keep longer with dry herbs.

Hot or Cold Asparagus Soup

Small cups of this served icy cold on a hot day or warm and creamy on a cold day are welcome. You can also garnish it with small cooked shrimp.

1. Using a large, heavy-bottomed soup pot, sauté the shallots in olive oil. When the shallots are softened, add the asparagus and toss for a few minutes.

2. Add the broth, salt, pepper, lemon juice and zest, and Tabasco. Cover and cook until the asparagus is very tender.

3. Whirl in the blender until very smooth. If you are going to serve it hot, reheat, add cream, and serve. For a cold soup, chill, add cream, and serve. Garnish with chopped fresh chives or mint leaves.

Makes about 15 cups

4 shallots, chopped
2 tablespoons olive oil
2 pounds fresh asparagus or 3 (10-ounce) packages frozen, cut into 1-inch pieces
2 quarts GF chicken broth
Salt and pepper to taste
Juice of 1 lemon, and 1 teaspoon lemon zest
1 teaspoon Tabasco sauce, or to taste
2 cups heavy cream
½ cup chopped fresh chives or mint leaves, for garnish

Tiny Garbanzo Crepes

Serves 12 as an appetizer

2 cups chickpea (garbanzo)
    flour
2 cloves garlic, crushed
1 teaspoon Tabasco sauce or
    other red hot sauce
1 teaspoon salt or to taste
1½ cups water
Olive oil as needed for cooking
    the crepes

These have a nutlike flavor that really works with lots of dips and fillings. You can make them in various sizes, depending on your party size.

1. Mix everything but the oil in a blender, pulsing and scraping down the side of the jar.

2. Heat some oil in a nonstick pan. Add 1 tablespoon of the batter for 1½-inch crepes.

3. Cook until very crisp on the bottom; do not turn. Remove from heat and keep on paper towels or a platter. Now you can add fillings of your choice and close, or fold in half and dip into a sauce.

Rich in Soluble Fiber

Nutritionists say garbanzo beans are rich in soluble fiber, which is the best type of fiber, actually helping to eliminate cholesterol from the body. Garbanzo beans are a good source of folate, vitamin E, potassium, iron, manganese, copper, zinc, and calcium. As a high-potassium, low-sodium food, they help reduce blood pressure.

Cheese Fondue with Dipping Vegetables

This is an "interactive" party appetizer, or you can serve it as a main course.

1. Mash the garlic, and in a large earthenware pot or chafing dish over a burner, heat the garlic in the wine.

2. Stir in the cheese, nutmeg, pepper, kirsch, and salt. Mix slowly over low flame.

3. In a separate bowl, whisk together the egg yolks, flour, and cream. Stir into the cheese mixture.

4. Serve with buttered bread cubes and vegetables, keeping the heat low under the chafing dish water basin. Or if you are using a heavy flameproof earthenware casserole, keep a low flame under it.

5. When the cheese mixture has melted, enjoy by spearing veggies or GF bread onto a long-handled fork and dipping into the cheese mixture. If the cheese gets too thick, add a bit more warm white wine.

Fondue Facts

Ever wonder where fondue came from? It was created in Switzerland, where it was used as a way of using up hardened cheese. Traditionally a peasant dish, fondue became popular in America in the 1950s, as a result of chef Konrad Egli's Chalet Swiss restaurant fondue. Later on came chocolate fondue.

Serves 12 to 14

1 clove garlic
1 cup dry white wine
1 pound imported Swiss cheese, such as Jarlsberg, coarsely grated
¼ teaspoon ground nutmeg
Freshly ground pepper to taste
3 tablespoons kirsch (liqueur)
Salt to taste
2 egg yolks, beaten
2 tablespoons gluten-free flour, such as potato flour
½ cup cream
2 tablespoons butter
1 loaf GF French-style bread, cubed and toasted
1 broccoli crown, blanched in boiling water for 2 minutes, cooled, and cut in pieces
2 sweet red peppers, cored, seeded, and cut into chunks
½ pound sugar snap peas, rinsed
2 zucchini and/or 12 very thin asparagus tips, cut up

Grilled Eggplant and Pepper Salad

Serves 12

⅓ cup balsamic or red wine vinegar
1 cup olive oil
1 teaspoon Dijon-style mustard
Salt and pepper to taste
1 medium eggplant, peeled and sliced in ½-inch rounds
3 red bell peppers, cored and seeded, cut in half
1 bunch arugula or watercress, stems removed, washed
1 large head romaine lettuce, washed, dried, and chopped
4 ripe tomatoes, cored and chopped
2 ounces aged provolone cheese

Grill the eggplant and peppers the day before the party, then, at the last minute, put the vegetables together, shave the provolone, and dress the salad.

1. To prepare the dressing, mix the first five ingredients together in a cruet. Shake well. Cut the eggplant into ½-inch slices, brush with salad dressing, and grill for 3 minutes on each side. Cool and cut into cubes.

2. Grill the peppers on the skin side until charred. Place in a paper bag. Cool and pull the skin off. Cut into pieces.

3. Just before serving, toss the greens with the eggplant and peppers, add tomatoes, and shave the provolone over the top.

4. Whirl the vinegar, oil, mustard, salt, and pepper in your blender. Pour over the salad.

Paella

You need a really big pan for this—you can get paella pans made of heavy metal that has been coated with enamel.

1. Preheat the oven to 350°F.

2. Brown the chicken and chorizo in the olive oil and push them to the side of the pan. Add the onion, garlic, and rice, stirring to soften the onion and garlic and coat the rice.

3. Add the broth, saffron, and tomatoes. Mix well.

4. Bake in a preheated oven at 350°F for 20 minutes or until the rice begins to take up the broth. Add the peas.

5. The order in which you add the seafood is crucial. Always put the ones that take the longest to cook in first, adding the more tender pieces at the end. Start by arranging the clams on top. When they start to open, add the mussels. When both are open, add the shrimp and simply mix them into the rice—shrimp take only 2 to 3 minutes to cook. Sprinkle with parsley and serve in the cooking pan.

Different Regions, Different Paellas

Different regions of Spain use different ingredients in their paella. Here in the United States, you may find lobster rather than langostini in paella, and we always use lots of clams.

Serves 10 to 16

2 chickens cut into 10 pieces
1 pound chorizo (Spanish sausage) or sweet Italian sausage, cut into bite-sized pieces
½ cup olive oil
1 large onion, diced
2 cloves garlic, minced
3 cups rice
5½ cups GF chicken broth
Pinch saffron
2 tomatoes, cored and chopped
1 10 ounce box tiny frozen peas (petit pois)
18 littleneck clams, scrubbed
18 mussels, scrubbed and debearded
1½ pounds jumbo shrimp, peeled and deveined
½ cup chopped fresh parsley

Stuffed, Roasted Filet Mignon

Serves 10 to 12

1 pound fresh spinach, washed, cut up, blanched, and squeezed to remove extra moisture, or 2 (10-ounce) boxes frozen spinach, thawed and drained
2 tablespoons olive oil
4 cloves garlic, minced
Juice of ½ lemon
¼ teaspoon nutmeg
1 cup GF soft bread crumbs mixed with seasonings such as dried oregano and salt and pepper to taste
1 6-pound filet mignon, well trimmed
1 teaspoon salt and freshly ground black pepper to taste
2 tablespoons softened butter
1 (13-ounce) can low-salt beef broth

This can be served hot, cold, or at room temperature. The garlic and spinach stuffing is a terrific counterpoint to the meat.

1. Preheat the oven to 350°F.

2. Place the spinach on paper towels to dry a bit. Heat the olive oil and add the garlic; cook over medium heat to soften. Mix in the spinach, lemon juice, and nutmeg, stirring. Add the bread crumbs.

3. Using a fat knitting needle or the handle of a dull knife, make a channel through the meat. Force in the stuffing.

4. Sprinkle the meat with salt and pepper, then rub with the softened butter. Roast in oven for 60 minutes, basting every 15 minutes with the beef broth. Reserve pan juice for another use. Let the filet rest for 15 minutes before serving.

Alternatives to Bread Crumbs

Try using your food processor to make crumbs of such goodies as cornbread, potato chips, or popcorn. Check various rice cereals such as puffed rice and rice crisps to make sure they are gluten-free, then put them in your food processor to make crumbs. Store the crumbs in resealable plastic bags in the refrigerator.

Chocolate-Dipped Strawberries

This crowd-pleaser is always delicious and is good to make in advance. Make sure to purchase the best strawberries you can find.

1. Rinse the berries and allow them to dry on paper towels.

2. Melt the chocolate and sugar in a double boiler over simmering water. Remove from heat.

3. Carefully dip the strawberries, one at a time, in the chocolate. Store in a cool place, or if made more than five hours ahead of time, store in the refrigerator.

A Valentine's Treat

One of the most popular Valentine's Day gifts is chocolate-dipped strawberries, with their bloom of red along with creamy or dark chocolate. Surprise your loved one with a homemade rendition that will melt his or her heart.

Makes 36 berries

36 very large strawberries with long stems
8 ounces bittersweet chocolate
6 ounces milk chocolate candy bars
4 ounces sugar

Dark Chocolate, Walnut, and Hazelnut Torte

Serves 14

1 pound bittersweet chocolate, chopped
1 cup unsalted butter, cut into pieces
¼ cup pure cocoa powder
¼ cup hazelnut liqueur
½ teaspoon vanilla extract
5 eggs
2 teaspoons orange zest, freshly scraped from a thick-skinned orange
1 cup hazelnuts, toasted, skinned, and ground
1 cup walnuts, toasted and ground
½ cup confectioners' sugar

This is exceedingly rich and delicious. Garnish with coffee or vanilla ice cream. A few fresh raspberries on the side are also an excellent counterpoint.

1. Preheat oven to 350°F. In the top of a double boiler, heat the chocolate and butter until chocolate melts. Remove from heat and stir.

2. Add cocoa powder, liqueur, vanilla, eggs, and orange zest, mixing well.

3. Add hazelnuts and walnuts and mix. Pour batter into greased 9-inch cake pan lined with parchment. Bake until cake is barely set, about 25 to 30 minutes.

4. Cool in the pan for 20 minutes. Remove from pan and place on a rack.

5. Cool completely and sprinkle with confectioners' sugar. Add raspberries and ice cream for garnish.

Vanilla

Whatever you do, don't use imitation vanilla extract—the pure stuff is a bit more expensive, but it tastes so much better it's worth it. Imitation vanilla extract may give food a slight chemical flavor. You can use vanilla beans to make flavored sugar: simply slit open a bean and place it in a jar with 2 cups sugar, seal, and let sit for a week.

Raw Veggies with Chili-Cheddar-Cheese Dip

Raw Veggies with Cheese Dip

Deep-Fried Chicken Wings

Italian Sausages on Quartered Sweet Peppers

Spaghetti Squash with Marinara Sauce and Cheese

Spaghetti Squash Mac 'n' Cheese

Homemade Potato Chips

Fresh Three-Berry Granita

Frozen Bananas Dipped in Chocolate

Jelly Bean Surprise Ice Cream

Molten Chocolate Chestnut Cake

Brownie Sundae

A Gluten-Free Party for Kids

chapter seventeen

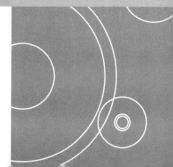

Raw Veggies with Chili-Cheddar-Cheese Dip

Makes 2 cups

Mixed raw vegetables such as carrots, celery, and green and yellow sweet peppers

2 tablespoons butter or margarine

2 tablespoons cornstarch or corn flour

1 cup warm milk

1½ cups grated Cheddar cheese

1 tablespoon onion powder

1 tablespoon chili powder, or to taste

1 tablespoon paprika

This is good for a fall or winter birthday party; it's fun to eat with crisp celery, carrots, or strips of red pepper. Kids of all ages love it.

1. Prepare the vegetables and place them in a plastic bag in the refrigerator.

2. Melt the butter and stir in the cornstarch or corn flour. Whisk in the milk; cook until thick. Add the rest of the ingredients, stir well, and serve with the veggies.

Raw Veggies with Cheese Dip

This is great for kids and adults; add spice as your taste buds dictate.

Whirl everything but the vegetables in the food processor, stopping occasionally to scrape the sides of the bowl. Refrigerate or serve immediately. Serve surrounded by veggies.

Going for the Crunch

Everybody loves crunchy foods, especially kids. And when dipped in wonderful hot and/or cold cheese sauces, vegetables are even better. This is a great way to get greens such as raw broccoli, sugar snap peas, and scallions into children. Of course, carrots and celery are standard, but try some red and/or yellow peppers to up the vitamins.

Makes 2 cups

4 ounces cream cheese, at room temperature
4 ounces blue or Gorgonzola cheese, at room temperature
½ cup GF mayonnaise
½ cup GF sour cream
1 teaspoon celery salt
Freshly ground black pepper to taste
Platter of raw vegetables

Deep-Fried Chicken Wings

Makes 20 wings

20 chicken wings, halved and
    trimmed, rinsed, and laid
    out on paper towels
1½ cups chickpea flour
1 teaspoon baking soda
1 teaspoon garlic powder
1½ cups water
1 egg
Salt and pepper to taste
Vegetable oil for frying, about
    2 quarts

Adjust the quantities to whatever else you are serving and to the size/ages of the kids attending the party. Use 10 to 12 wings for each teenager, and 4 to 5 for each kinder-gartner.

1. Be sure to dry the rinsed chicken pieces thoroughly on paper towels.

2. Mix the flour, baking soda, garlic powder, water, egg, salt, and pepper in the blender until smooth. Pour into a large bowl.

3. Heat the oil to 350°F. Dip the wings, 3 or 4 at a time, in the batter and, using tongs, place them in the hot oil. Fry for 20 minutes.

4. Drain on paper towels. Keep warm in a low (200°F) oven if you make the wings in advance. Serve with hot sauce on the side for older kids.

A Trade Secret

To turn fried wings into Buffalo wings, named after that big old town in upstate New York, mix ½ pound butter, 2 teaspoons cider vinegar, and hot sauce to taste in a saucepan over medium heat. When the butter is melted, dip the wings into the sauce, to heat and flavor.

Italian Sausages on Quartered Sweet Peppers

A little sausage goes a long way. Use the sweet sausage for young kids; older ones may like hot sausages.

1. Place whole sausages in a pot with water to cover, then bring to a rolling boil. Reduce the heat and simmer for 10 minutes.

2. Remove sausages from water. Grill on high heat until nicely browned all over. Cut in rounds and serve on "spoons" of red or green pepper.

Secrets of Italian Sausage

A top-notch Italian sausage will have little fat, so little, in fact, that you may have to add oil to the frying pan when you cook it. In making meatballs, mix ½ pound of the sausage with the meat for the meatballs and you will be surprised at the difference.

Makes 16 sausage rounds

1 pound Italian sausages, hot or sweet

4 large sweet red or green peppers, cored, seeded, and cut into quarters

Spaghetti Squash with Marinara Sauce and Cheese

Serves 6 to 8

1 4-pound spaghetti squash, rinsed

1 cup freshly grated Parmesan cheese

Garnish of fresh herbs such as parsley, basil, and oregano

2 cups of your favorite jarred, GF marinara sauce

Spaghetti squash holds endless possibilities for a nutritious, gluten-free diet. It's delicious and so easy to prepare.

1. Preheat oven to 275°F.

2. Make a boat of aluminum foil and place the squash in the center. Pierce the squash in several places with a knife to let the steam escape. Sprinkle with water. Tent with more foil and roast for 2 hours. The squash is done when you can insert a fork easily.

3. Cool the squash so you can handle it. Cut it in half and scoop out the seeds. Using a fork, run it through the flesh and it will turn into spaghetti.

4. Mix the squash and most of the cheese together and reheat. Sprinkle with the remaining cheese and herbs, toss with marinara, and serve.

Freshly Grated Cheese

Blocks of Parmesan cheese will keep for a week, tightly wrapped, in the refrigerator. It is so easy to grate exactly the amount you need, when you need it, and it tastes 100 percent better than the grated cheese you get in a box or jar. Use a box grater and place a piece of waxed paper on your board. Grate away, then remove the grater, make a funnel of the paper, and slide the cheese into a bowl or add it to what you are preparing. You can also use Romano, Fontina, or Cheddar cheese in this way and enjoy them so much more.

Spaghetti Squash Mac 'n' Cheese

Everybody loves macaroni and cheese. This recipe substitutes spaghetti squash for the mac and uses Chili-Cheddar-Cheese Dip.

1. Preheat oven to 275°F.

2. Make a boat of aluminum foil and place the squash in the center. Pierce the squash in several places with a knife to let the steam escape. Sprinkle with water. Tent with more foil and roast for 2 hours. The squash is done when you can insert a fork easily.

3. Cool the squash so you can handle it. Prepare a 10-inch glass baking pan with nonstick spray. Using a fork, make "spaghetti" of the squash and scrape it into the baking pan.

4. Increase temperature of oven to 350°F.

5. Mix the sauce and extra milk into the baking pan. Sprinkle the extra cheese on top and dot with butter. Bake for 30 minutes, until hot and bubbling.

Serves 4 to 6

1 5-pound spaghetti squash, rinsed
1 recipe for Chili-Cheddar-Cheese Dip (see page 284)
½ cup milk
1½ cups extra grated Cheddar cheese for topping
2 tablespoons butter

Homemade
Potato Chips

Makes about 75 chips

4 large Yukon Gold potatoes
2 quarts light vegetable oil,
    such as canola
Salt to taste

These are just too good and will be grabbed up fast, so plan to make extra.

1. Peel and slice the potatoes. The best way to slice these chips is with a mandolin or the slicing blade on your food processor.

2. Place 2 inches of oil in the fryer. Heat the oil to 340°F and watch the temperature throughout the cooking time.

3. Carefully add potato slices, a few at a time, to hot oil. Remove when golden and drain on brown paper bags or paper towels. Sprinkle with salt. Serve hot or warm. (For a variation, mix 2 teaspoons chili powder with 2 teaspoons salt and sprinkle on the chips as they cool.)

Fresh Three-Berry Granita

This is fine as is or mixed with vanilla ice cream. The more varieties of fruit you use, the better.

1. Mix the sugar and water together in a large saucepan and bring to a boil. Reduce heat and simmer until all of the sugar is dissolved.

2. Add the rinsed and stemmed berries and cook for 6 minutes. Add the lemon juice.

3. Place in your freezer in ice trays. Occasionally break up the granita with a fork so that it does not turn into a block of ice. Or use an ice cream freezer to make your granita. The ice cream freezer will increase the shelf life of the granita, making it a sorbet. Soften slightly before serving.

Makes 1 quart

1½ cups sugar
⅔ cups water
1 pint strawberries, rinsed, stems removed
1½ pints fresh raspberries, rinsed
½ pint fresh blueberries, rinsed and picked over
¼ cup lemon juice

Frozen Bananas
Dipped in Chocolate

Serves 10

10 bananas
10 Popsicle sticks
1 pound semisweet chocolate
2 cups sugar, or to taste
Pinch salt
1 teaspoon pure vanilla extract

Kids love these and so do lots of grownups. They're a snap to make, and you can involve the older kids in the dipping.

1. Peel the bananas and insert the Popsicle sticks. Place bananas on a cookie sheet you have prepared with nonstick spray and freeze.

2. Just before serving, melt the chocolate and sugar in a large saucepan. Add the salt and vanilla. Let cool to warm but not harden.

3. Dip the frozen bananas into the chocolate and place on waxed paper. The frozen bananas will harden the chocolate, and they're ready to eat right away.

Jelly Bean Surprise Ice Cream

This is great for little kids—just say, "Surprise!" and they get happy.

Partially thaw the ice cream. Mix in the jelly-beans. Refreeze and serve.

A President's Passion

Everyone knows that former president Ronald Reagan was renowned for his love of jelly beans. After the president's death, the Jelly Belly candy company created black ribbons made out of jelly beans, in his memory.

Makes 6 cups

1 quart vanilla ice cream
1½ cups of the smallest jelly beans you can find

Molten Chocolate Chestnut Cake

Serves 10 to 12

1 cup chestnut flour
1 cup rice flour
1 tablespoon xanthan gum
¾ cup cocoa powder
2 teaspoons baking powder
Pinch salt
8 ounces unsalted butter
1¼ cups sugar
1½ cups sour cream
2 eggs
GF vanilla or chocolate ice
cream to fill the center

The grownups will love this too. Fill the hole with vanilla ice cream and sprinkle with chocolate bits or M&Ms.

1. Preheat the oven to 350°F. Prepare a bundt pan with nonstick spray.

2. Sift into a bowl the two flours, xanthan gum, cocoa powder, baking powder, and salt.

3. Place butter and sugar in a large bowl. Using an electric mixer on low, mix until creamed and light. Add half the flour/cocoa mixture and beat until well incorporated.

4. Add the sour cream and the eggs and mix vigorously. Slowly add the rest of the flour/cocoa mixture and beat until you are sure there are no lumps.

5. Stop the mixer to scrape the bowl. Pour the batter into the bundt pan and bake for 1 hour. The cake will be soft and custardy. Just before serving, fill with ice cream.

Chocolate and Other Goodies

Chocolate and chestnuts are a marriage made in heaven. Most nuts marry well with chocolate. You could substitute almond flour for chestnut flour in this recipe. Chocolate and coffee are divine together, as are chocolate and raspberries, strawberries, or bananas. There's much to be said for combinations of chocolate and vanilla, chocolate and mint, and milk chocolate with dark chocolate. Experiment—you can't go wrong.

Brownie Sundae

When you crumble warm brownies over vanilla, chocolate, or coffee ice cream, you have something delicious.

1. Preheat oven to 300°F. Spray an 8" x 8" baking pan with nonstick spray.

2. Melt the chocolate and butter together over low heat. Whisk in the sugar.

3. Mix together the egg, flour, baking powder, and vanilla. Then stir in chocolate mixture. Spread on the bottom of the prepared baking pan. Bake for about 30 minutes.

4. Cool for 5 minutes. Crumble and serve over bowls of ice cream.

Chocolate Sauce

When you make a thick chocolate sauce, you need to remember that it is best made with real chocolate blocks, not with cocoa. When you melt the chocolate, you can use a heavy pan or the top of a double boiler. If necessary, you can add a teaspoon of butter or water to the chocolate.

Serves 8

3 ounces bittersweet chocolate
½ stick (¼ cup) butter or margarine
1 cup sugar
1 egg
⅔ cup rice flour
1 teaspoon GF baking powder
1 teaspoon vanilla
1 quart GF ice cream, flavor of choice

Keys to a
Gluten-Free Diet

appendix a

According to the Gluten Intolerance Group *(www.gluten.net)* and the American Dietetic Association, the following grains, flours, and starches are allowed in a gluten-free diet:

- Arrowroot
- Amaranth
- Quinoa
- Millet
- Teff
- Nut

The following grains contain gluten and are *not* allowed:

- Wheat (durum, semolina)
- Wheat bran, germ, starch
- Rye
- Barley
- Bran
- Bulgur
- Cereal binding
- Couscous
- Einkorn
- Emmer
- Farro
- Filler (unspecified)
- Graham flour
- Malt products derived from barley
- Orzo
- Spelt
- Triticale
- Kamut
- Farina
- Oats/Oat bran

The following ingredients are questionable and should not be consumed unless you can verify that they neither contain nor are derived from prohibited grains:

- Brown rice syrup (frequently made with barley)
- Caramel color (usually corn, but can be derived from wheat)
- Dextrin (usually corn, but may be derived from wheat)
- Flour or cereal products
- Hydrolyzed vegetable protein (HVP), hydrolyzed plant protein (HPP), unless they specify an acceptable ingredient
- Textured vegetable protein (TVP)
- Malt, malt vinegar, or malt flavoring (usually made from barley; okay if made from corn)
- Modified food starch or modified starch from prohibited source
- Mono- and di-glycerides (in dry products only)
- Natural and artificial flavors (However, extracts such as vanilla, orange, and lemon are gluten-free.)
- Seasonings
- Starches

Additional items frequently overlooked which often contain gluten:

- Breading
- Coating mixes
- Communion wafers
- Croutons
- Imitation bacon
- Imitation seafood
- Marinades
- Pastas
- Processed meats
- Roux
- Sauces
- Self-basting poultry
- Soup bases
- Stuffing
- Thickeners

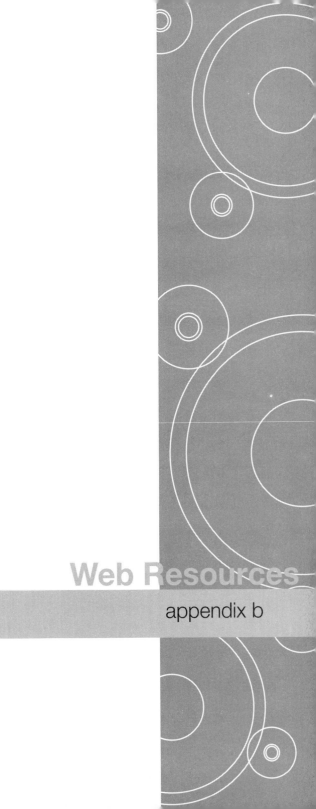

Web Resources

appendix b

The Gluten-Free Mall
www.glutenfreemall.com

The Gluten-Free Mall was created by Scott Adams, who is better known in the celiac/gluten-free community for founding Celiac.com. On this site, you'll find high-quality gluten-free products.

The George Mateljan Foundation for the World's Healthiest Foods
www.whfoods.com

The George Mateljan Foundation for the World's Healthiest Foods was established by George Mateljan to discover, develop, and share scientifically proven information about the benefits of healthy eating. You can use the site's Recipe Assistant to search for recipes that exclude certain foods.

The Gluten Intolerance Group
www.gluten.net

The Gluten Intolerance Group, also known as GIG, is a 501(c)(3) nonprofit organization funded by private donations, including the Combined Federal Campaign, United Way Designated Giving, Employer Matching Funds, proceeds from memberships, and the sale of products and educational resources.

Living Without
www.livingwithout.com

Living Without is a lifestyle guide for people with allergies and food sensitivities. It discusses a wide variety of health issues, including allergies; food sensitivities; multiple chemical sensitivities; wheat intolerance; gluten intolerance; lactose intolerance; dairy allergies; eating disorders; asthma; diabetes; dermatitis; gastroenterology-related disorders; diets that heal; celiac disease; anaphylaxis; and the common allergens of egg, dairy, wheat, peanuts, tree nuts, shellfish, fish, corn, soy, and gluten.

Gluten Freeda
www.glutenfreeda.com

The Glutenfreeda program was created to help people with celiac sprue disease learn to prepare all the foods they love, gluten-free. Their goal is to show the gluten-intolerant how to eat well, eat healthy, and function happily in a gluten-engorged world. Glutenfreeda recipes will be enjoyed by your entire family and were selected to make eating a delicious experience, not a sacrifice.

Cooking Gluten-Free!
www.cookingglutenfree.com
Published by Celiac Publishing, Cooking Gluten-Free! is a labor of love designed to prove that gluten-free food can be excellent.

Rice and Recipes
www.riceandrecipes.com
Recipes, recipe contests, rice links, rice facts.

Gluten-Free Pantry
www.glutenfreepantry.com
Recipes; retail-store locator; information on celiac disease, autism, and more.

Celiac Disease and Gluten-Free Diet Support Center
www.celiac.com/celiacdisease.html
This support center at Celiac.com provides important resources and information for people on gluten-free diets due to celiac disease, gluten intolerance, dermatitis herpetiformis, wheat allergy, or other health issues. Celiac.com offers key gluten- and wheat-free online resources that are helpful to anyone with special dietary needs.

The Gluten Free Trio
www.pamelasproducts.com/GFTrio.html
The Gluten Free Trio is a collaboration of three independent companies: Pamela's Products, Mrs. Leeper's Pasta, and Edward & Sons.

Gluten Solutions
www.glutensolutions.com
Buy food, get information, join the Web ring.

Amazing Grains
www.amazinggrains.com
This site sells Montina flour, cookbooks, and bakeware, and also features a grower's co-op and support groups.

features a grower's co-op and support groups.

Enjoy Life Foods
www.enjoylifefoods.com
Browse and buy, food facts, resources.

Gluten-Free InfoWeb
www.glutenfreeinfo.com/Diet/glutenfreeinfo.htm
Check out which brand-name food products are gluten-free. Search food lists, check out their bookstore, and join their InfoList to receive a free newsletter.

Index